THE PSYCHOLOGY OF EDUCATION

*A Theoretical Approach
in Child Development*

Copyright © 2011 by Velma Melancon
Los Angeles, California

All Rights Reserved
Printed and Bound in the United States of America

Published and Distribted by: Professional Publishing House
1425 W. Manchester Ave., Suite B Los Angeles, CA 90047
www.professionalpublishinghouse.com

drrosie@aol.com
323-750-3592

Cover Design: George Hooks

Second Printing, February 2013
10 9 8 7 6 5 4 3 2 1
ISBN 978-0-9834444-3-5
Library of Congress Control Number: 2013932780

Publisher's Note
All rights reserved. No part of this book may be reproduced in whole or in part, in any form or by any means, electronic or mechanical, including photocopying, recording or by any information storage and retrieval system, without permission in writing from the author. Address inquiries to: velmamelancon@att.net

THE PSYCHOLOGY OF EDUCATION

A Theoretical Approach in Child Development

Velma Melancon, M.A., Ed.

Acknowledgments

I am especially grateful to my children, Dennis and Patricia, and grandchildren, Demitre and Jonathan, who were the real-life inspirations for me writing this book. Their love, encouragement, and enthusiasm provided me with the support needed to continue. Someday, they'll know how much they helped me.

I would also like to express my gratitude to my friends and colleagues, who, through their unusual vision, intelligence, and learning, helped me clarify my thinking about child development.

Finally, thank you for the additional support from a very personal friend whom I love and respect dearly, who prayed with me throughout this process with much love and remained faithful.

—Velma Melancon

About the Author

VELMA MELANCON IS A FORMER associate professor at Los Angeles Southwest College. She has been an elementary teacher in the Lynwood Unified School District. Her credentials include a master of arts degree with a major in education and a bachelor of arts degree with a major in sociology and a minor in early childhood studies from the California State University Dominguez Hills.

Ms. Melancon has an associate of arts degree in liberal arts studies from Los Angeles Southwest College. She also has a standard teaching credential K through 3 in early childhood education and a standard teaching credential K through 9 and a California community colleges credential in nursery and preschool education.

As an associate professor, Velma Melancon has taught child development courses at the Los Angeles Southwest Community College District and at Drew University in Los Angeles, California. Ms. Melancon has been an elementary school teacher in the Lynwood Unified School District for over two decades.

She is listed in Who's Who Among American Teachers, Second Edition, Volume 2, 1992. She is especially interested in intellectual development from childhood through adolescence.

Her major research focus deals with cognitive development and factors that contribute to the maintenance of intellectual functioning, not only its structure, but how people process information, the nature of intelligence, and human language. It includes what psychologists know about family life, social relations, and understanding personality. Her expertise also covers physical growth and emotions, the history of the field, topics of heredity and environment, personality, moral development, and becoming an individual.

Table of Contents

ACKNOWLEDGMENTS 5
ABOUT THE AUTHOR 7
PREFACE 11
INTRODUCTION 15
Chapter 1: The History and Study of Child Development:
   Theories in the Twentieth Century 19
Chapter 2: Literature and Critical Thinking 31
Chapter 3: A Comparison of Theories of Child Development
   in the Twentieth Century............................... 45
Chapter 4: The Middle Twentieth-Century Theories of
   Childhood: An introduction to Dewey, Montessori,
   Erikson, Piaget, and Vygotsky........................... 51
Chapter 5: A Comparison of Studies in Behavior Modification
   and Piaget's Theory of Cognitive Development 53
Chapter 6: Stages of Reflexive Behavior 69
Chapter 7: Preparing Educators to Work with
   Students from Diverse Backgrounds 79
Chapter 8: Methods of Psychological Research
   and Psychological Assessment 87
Chapter 9: Lesson Plan Samples 95
Chapter 10: The Development of Motives and
   Values in the Child.................................... 133
Chapter 11: Ethnic Diversity and Contemporary Families....... 145

Chapter 12: The Future of Learning into the
    Twenty-First Century.................................... 147
Chapter 13: Learn English as a Second Language................ 159
Chapter 14: Effective Practices and Principles to Support English
    Language Learners in the Early Childhood Classroom 161
Chapter 15: "The Culture of Teaching" 163
Chapter 16: Teacher Portfolios 173
Chapter 17: Teaching and Learning Experiences in
    Early Childhood Education................................ 179
Chapter 18: The Challenge for Early Childhood Education
    in the Twenty-First Century 189
GLOSSARY 197
REFERENCES 210
FURTHER READINGS 211
INDEX 217
APPENDIX 223

Preface

THIS BOOK IS WRITTEN FOR parents, students, those who wish to become teachers, administrators, those who wish or need to know about young children, as well as for those who are interested in their own children and how they develop socially and intellectually.

My goal for this book is to describe the growth and development of preschool and early childhood education. This book is intended to be an introduction to child development based on the theory and research from the beginning of its early history from the late nineteenth and early twentieth century.

One of the first to do research in this field was G. Stanley Hall, an American psychologist who got his Ph.D. at Harvard and later taught at Clark University. Today, the majority of people who are doing research in this field consider themselves psychologists or developmental psychologists. Many of these people are college professors, members of psychology departments in colleges and universities all over the world. Some are associated with other university departments (biology or sociology, for example), or with schools of education, or medicine, or nursing.

All of these people are unified in their interest in young children. They find children fascinating and want to find out more about their development and desire to tell others about what they have learned.

The results of research on child development are made public in several different ways. The most common way is to write a report describing the research and its results, and to submit it to one of the journals that publish scientific papers on these topics.

Much of the work that I will be describing in this book originally appeared in journals like Child Development, Developmental Psychology, and the Journal of Experimental Child Psychology. Issues of these journals appear several times a year, and each issue generally contains between 10 to 40 papers on child development. The authors of these papers have carried out a research project, done some statistical analysis of their results, written a concise report (in the style and format demanded by these journals) describing what they did and what they found out, and submitted their report to a journal.

The journal editor then sends copies of this paper to two or three reviewers, usually college professors who have done research of a similar nature to that reported in the paper. These reviewers give their opinions: that the research reported in the paper is interesting and competently done and that the paper should be published as is, or that the research is of insufficient interest or quality and that the paper should not be published, or that the research has merit but the paper needs to be revised in some way before it can be published.

In any case, whenever I state that some piece of information comes from a specific source, I will provide information about that source. The names and dates in parentheses you'll find scattered throughout the text can be looked up in the reference list at the back of this book. If I make a factual statement and it doesn't have a reference after it, it's because I am summarizing results distilled from many other sources, not just one or two that will be listed in the references at the back of the book.

True "educating societies" are ones in which teachers, too, can continue to learn, and there must be a serious commitment to their learning in both time and energy with thousands of students.

My purpose of writing this book is to communicate to readers the great variety in educational and psychological thinking about young children as we enter into the twenty-first century.

I have attempted to maintain a consistent research perspective. I decided to draw heavily upon the technical details of empirical investigations in early childhood education research activity with full recognition that some readers may not be familiar with the style and technical details of the research activity.

It is conceivable that some readers may wish to skip the segments of this book that concern research reviews. If so, I trust that such readers will not disregard the importance of children's measured behavior introduced in this book in terms of issues that are the basis to strategies in early childhood education, both individually and collectively. The reader will see these various complex issues are largely grounded in psychological theory, philosophy, and sociocultural values and ethics.

Introduction

THE STUDY OF CHILD development deals with the growth and maturation process of children—physical, mental, emotional, and social. This subject is important to all those involved with children—parents, teachers, medical professionals, and social policy makers, among others, as well as to anyone interested in understanding people in general.

Theories about the nature of children have undergone much change, especially in the last three centuries. Some of the most influential thinkers in this area were Comenius, Locke, Rousseau, Froebel, Darwin, and Dewey. Because of the ideas of such people, we no longer accept the medieval view of children as miniature adults, but appreciate children for themselves. We generally agree that they require special care and education and that they are deeply influenced by their environment, especially their homes and schools.

The earliest studies of children were biographies of specific babies—not very scientific according to modern standards. Current child development research has two major goals: to catalog and describe how children behave at various ages, and to understand why they behave the way they do. Modern investigators conduct their research in a systematic manner, using methods similar to those used in the physical sciences.

Some of the major issues and trends in current studies relate to these questions:

- Does individual development repeat the stages of the evolution of the species?
- What are the relative influences of heredity (nature) and environment (nurture)?
- What causes behavioral differences among various groups?
- What is the relationship between animal behavior and human behavior?
- Can human behavior be predicted?

Research design usually involves formulating a hypothesis, devising relevant variables, selecting experimental and control groups choosing subjects who will be a sample of the population to be studied, and devising appropriate methods of accumulating data. Studies may be experimental, corelational, clinical applied, done in the field, longitudinal, cross-sectional, cross-cultural, correlations, important products or research, or are statistical findings that measure the degree of correspondence between variables in the experiment.

Many legal and ethical problems must be confronted by human development investigators. Experimentation with human beings involves the special difficulties of preserving them from harm, obtaining their informed consent, and protecting their privacy. When the subjects are children who are particularly vulnerable because of their age, parental consent is essential. Despite these difficulties, a great deal of significant research has been accomplished, particularly in the past 50 years. These investigations provide the foundation of current knowledge of child development.

Some of the most eminent educators maintain that what is learned first lasts the longest and is less likely to eradicate.

INTRODUCTION

I have observed infants in early childhood education use their five senses to explore, discover, and learn about their world through stages of sensorimotor development, which is symbolic and without thought or language patterns.

In early infancy, young children reveal themselves through their behavior. Two scientists in this field, Seefeldt and Kellog, stated that early childhood education has turned to child observation in natural settings as the most effective means for assessing the learning development and behavior of infancy, preschool, and kindergarten children. All children go through a sequence of development that can be observed through their senses, from one-word utterances and to simple sentences.

The basis of this text helps observers to focus on the following three major areas which can be found in the early chapters:

- Defining educational psychology and develop methods of teaching
- How children learn
- An introduction to theories of early childhood
- John Dewey
- Maria Montessori
- Erik Erikson
- Jean Piaget
- Lev Vygotsky

These theories are divided into six important chapters of child development. Each chapter expands on the developmental sequences or stages based on recognized developmental sequence.

Some of the characteristics that describe stages of observed behavior in early childhood development are social, emotional, and intellectual or cognitive.

The senses in early infancy are used by infants to explore their environment and their interactions within their environment. Piaget believes the most effective tool for assessment in infancy is studied through observation because young children are unable to express themselves fully with words. Therefore, they reveal themselves through their behaviors.

Early childhood specialist Carolyn Seefeldt agrees that "observing is probably, the oldest, most frequently used and most rewarding method of assessing children, their growth, development, and learning." She further states that young children are incapable of hiding their feelings, ideas, or emotions with socially approved behaviors; therefore, observing them often yields accurate information.

Teachers, caregivers, child observers, and parents who want to find out why a certain child is not getting along with others should spend time observing that child's interpersonal behaviors with peers.

This text looks at the sequence of a child's development. It uses an observation tool, the child skills checklist, to help teachers, caregiver child observers, and parents to determine where a child stands in various developmental sequences so that they may plan activities to further the child's growth.

The text goes by the sequence of child development in order to teach the nonspecialist to understand children through observing their developmental sequence in four major areas of child development: emotional, social, physical, and cognitive.

This textbook takes a different point of view instead of focusing on a great deal of assessment and evaluation of children today to determine how we can intervene to help him or her. It looks for answers to the questions: What's right with the young child? And how can we use his or her strengths to help in the development of the child?

Chapter 1

The History and Study of Child Development: Theories in the Twentieth Century

I WAS INFLUENCED THE MOST BY Piaget's work that was primarily in the area of stages of cognitive development; he paid little attention to children's emotions or motivations.

Piaget formulated his theory of cognitive development on the basis of observations of his own three children, testing specific hypothesis about how children think by observing them and by interviewing other children.

I like what Piaget said about his stage theory of cognitive development in observing the child the first 2 years of life. Piaget stated that the child has only a limited capacity to represent and comprehend knowledge about the world and, thus, to think. However, Piaget said that the child learns about the environment by constant activity, exploration, and manipulation.

I agree with Piaget's stage theory of development, where each successive stage is qualitatively distinct from the one that went before it, meaning that the transition from stage to stage may build on and incorporate elements from the earlier stage; and that learning occurs through activity, exploration, and manipulation of the environment, and motor and sensory impressions form the foundation of later learning.

This book begins with the history and study of child development in the 1970s, and theories of development in the 1980s. In the middle of the twentieth century, theories of child development and early twentieth century child psychology became a science.

The Subject Matter and Its Early History

Who is interested?

Parents seek guidance about how their children develop and how to cope with them while they are young. Teachers, nurses, doctors, social workers, and administrators, among others, all want information about the range of "normal" behavior of children at various ages. They also would like to know what conditions could create individual differences.

Many mothers and fathers would be pleased to be able to bring up children who are bright, creative, motivated, talented, loving, obedient, happy, and popular with the "right" kind of friends. Other parents would like their children to be able to fulfill their "ultimate potential." Teachers would be delighted to know the secret of producing a class full of pupils who learn readily, ask the right questions, strive to do well, and are never unruly. Nurses and doctors would be glad if they could precisely diagnose all behavioral and psychological problems brought to them and prescribe sure cures.

It would be a utopia (a visionary scheme or system for social policymakers) if the information were available to enable the authorities to set up schools and programs to transform all children in the United States into well educated, prosperous, informed voters.

Early ideas

Researchers who study human behavior would probably be happy to help everyone fulfill these assorted goals. For at least three centuries, some individuals have been trying systematically to understand the conditions that could influence the minds, personalities, and behavior of children.

Earlier, in the Middle Ages, infants were generally looked upon as unimportant creatures that required only physical care. As for children, they were treated like small adults who needed correction when they did not meet grown-up standards. This attitude began to change in the seventeenth century, when certain intellectual leaders asserted that children were not ready for adult life and needed schooling to prepare them for their roles in society. Families also began to be recognized as molders of bodies and souls. Both are concepts that we share today (Aries 1962).

John Amos Comenius was an influential seventeenth-century philosopher who pioneered the motion that material used in school should be on the level of the pupils' ability and interest. He was the creator of one of the first picture books for children. He thought, as modern scholars also do, that children learn through their senses.

Another of today's ideas that first came from Comenius is that children should not, and cannot, be forced to learn. Rather, they must want to learn. Therefore, he did not believe in punishing a child for failing to learn. He thought it was the teacher's responsibility to create the desire to learn and that a pleasant atmosphere is an important motivator.

John Locke, slightly later in the seventeenth century, may have been the earliest "environmentalist." He wrote that experience is the source of reason and knowledge. He believed that the child's mind is blank at birth and that environment—people and surroundings—provides ideas. Locke's theories led to our current conviction that children should be treated as rational individuals.

Jean-Jacques Rousseau, an eighteenth-century thinker, really "discovered" children. He wrote: "Nature wants children to be children before they are men. If we deliberately pervert this order, we shall get premature fruits which are neither ripe nor well-flavored, and which soon decay." He was the first intellectual leader to express concern about children's well-being and to urge consideration for the young. Rousseau rejected the idea of original sin. He thought children are born with natural goodness.

An intellectual descendant of Rousseau was Friedrich Fröebel, a nineteenth-century German educator. He invented the kindergarten. He believed that children as young as a year old could be encouraged to act spontaneously. By following their own interests, they would be able to "unfold" their "inner essence."

Some believe that Charles Darwin's mid-nineteenth-century work, On the *Origin of Species*, was the real beginning of the science of child behavior. Darwin originated the notion that human development can be understood only by a study of origins, and the origins of men and women are the children they once were (Kessen 1965).

John Dewey may have had the most profound influence on the study of children in the twentieth century. He contributed the idea that schools are society's most important institutions, places where civilization's fate is decided.

Earliest studies

Along with early theories about the nature of children came attempts to find out what children are like and how they develop. Perhaps the first systematic study was the diary kept by a doctor to record the development of King Louis XIII of France, born in 1601. It contained 9,000 entries, covering his first 26 years (Marvick 1974).

A later, slightly more sophisticated investigation was the "baby biography." The first was published in 1774 by Johann Pestalozzi, a Swiss educator, who observed his own baby son. He theorized about the nature of the child and how and why he grew as he did. Similar biographical studies followed, written by Dietrich Tiedemann, an eighteenth-century German philosopher, and Charles Darwin, among others.

Unfortunately, by modern scientific standards, these early investigations were seriously flawed. The material was gathered by no particular system. The authors' samples were limited to a single well-loved child. Each observer had his own pet theory to promote. These early studies were important in young children because they were forerunners of later scientific investigations of how children develop and the conditions that create individual differences.

Current Ideas and Research

Goals

The study of child development has come a long way since the diaries of two or three hundred years ago. Today, investigators follow rigorous, scientific standards in attempting to learn the facts about human behavior. They have two major goals: to catalog and describe how children act at various ages and to understand why they behave as they do. Since all adults were once children, to understand children is also to gain an understanding of the grown-ups they become.

Nevertheless, developmental psychology will probably never match the physical sciences in terms of precise answers to precise questions. Human behavior is inevitably full of uncontrollable exceptions and variables. Individuals are (by definition) different from one another; therefore, behavior is full of differences. Thus, "laws" of behavior can only be generalizations that apply to most people most of the time. As in any scientific effort, the purpose of the study of child development is to gain a fuller understanding of the world and the people in it. The practical goal is to describe; the theoretical goal is to explain.

Leading theorists

The first influential modern theory and investigation in the field of child development in this country came from G. Stanley Hall. Late in the nineteenth century, Hall began to study children in a systematic way. He believed that his work would lead to a better understanding of adults. His particular contribution was the use of questionnaires to be answered by large groups of children and parents.

Sigmund Freud, Jean Piaget, Erik Erikson, Abraham Maslow, and Carl Rogers are some of the major authors of current theories relating to stages of emotional and cognitive development. As a result of their work, it is now generally accepted that human development progresses in biologically based stages, linked in a continuum. What happens to an individual in one stage can influence behavior in subsequent stages. Modern investigators try to discover the behavior that is characteristic of particular age spans.

Arnold Gesell was a pioneer in working out behavioral norms-levels of behavior that seem to describe how most children act most of the time under given conditions. Norms are characteristics of a group, but they are not necessarily true for every individual in the group. Therefore, individual differences might also be normal.

B.F. Skinner, a spiritual descendant of John Locke, is an enormously influential advocate of environmentalism, a dominant theory in modern developmental psychology. Environmentalists believe that human behavior is shaped by outside influences we encounter in the course of our lives. Most of today's research attempts, in one way or another, to discover exactly how child behavior is affected by environment. It includes the conditions under which children are conceived and born and under which they are reared and educated; the mores of the group to which they belong; the family's lifestyle and relative poverty or wealth; the very air they breathe.

These are only some of the important names and dominant theories in modern child development research. The work of these leaders and other investigators will be described in later chapters. All the researchers have something in common: the systematic way in which they conduct their studies, in contrast to the informal and unsupported theorizing of past centuries.

The Role and Scope of Educational Psychology

The role of educational psychology in teacher education is based on the premise that there are general principles of meaningful classroom learning that can be derived from a plausible theory of such learning. These principles can be both empirically validated and effectively communicated to prospective teachers. They provide a psychological rationale for teachers both for discovering more efficacious teaching methods on their own and for choosing more intelligently among the new teaching methods that are constantly being thrust upon them. valid theories and methods of teaching must be related to the nature of the learning process in the classroom and to both the cognitive and the affective-social factors that influence it.

In the past, psychological principles of learning bore little or no relationship to actual classroom teaching because they were uncritically extrapolated from research on rote and animal learning (or from other simpler kinds of learning such as conditioning and instrumental learning), all of which are intrinsically unrelated to most subject matter learning.

In considering the role and scope of educational psychology in modern education, a number of important questions are to be considered.

1. What justification is there for advocating that educational psychology constitutes part of the preparation of all prospective teachers? Does knowledge of subject matter suffice in teaching a given subject effectively? Are teachers born rather than made?

2. What contributions can psychology make to education, or in what ways can psychological principles be applied to educational practice? Does educational psychology have anything to offer that is not implicit in commonsensical notions of teaching, and how do its legitimate concerns differ from those of psychology proper?

3. Why has classroom learning theory undergone a serious decline over the past half century? Is there room for both theories of learning and theories of teaching? If so, what should be the relationship between them?

4. What part does research strategy play in educational psychology? Is educational psychology established in its own right with its own basic theory, research problems, and methodology, or does it merely consist of the direct application of general psychological principles and methods to educational problems? Should research

workers in educational psychology follow a basic science or an applied approach?

5. Are there qualitatively different kinds of learning, or can all manifestations of learning be explained by the same basic principles? From the standpoint of what is learned in school, what distinctions are most helpful in classifying the various kinds of learning?

6. What are the principal factors influencing school learning, and what is the most useful way of categorizing them?

7. What current trends in educational psychology should focus primarily on the nature and facilitation of subject matter learning?

Educational psychologists are concerned with the relationship between teaching methods and the aspects of a learner's performance that are described by the objectives.

Research on teaching methods provide information about the effect that different methods have on student performance. There are two basic types of teaching methods most often used. Both methods of teaching individual students have become more widely used and studied as the result of the development of programmed instruction, teaching machines, and computer-assisted instruction.

The study of individual methods has led to a more detailed study of teaching methods in general. Previously, teaching methods were loosely described. They left too much to be filled in by the teacher using them. As a result, studies of methods were carried out in a variety of ways.

The educational psychologists provide teachers and curriculum specialists with principles to use in organizing instructional materials and in interpreting tests. When a teacher uses educational objectives to determine the content of instruction and tests, students' gains are meaningfully related to those objectives. For example, an achievement test can be used to test students both before and after they take part in an educational program. The difference between the test scores reveals the amount of learning the students have gained.

During the 1950s and 1960s, a group of psychologists, educators, and other specialists classified all the goals of learning. They divided educational objectives into three areas: (1) the cognitive area, (2) the psychomotor area, and (3) the affective area.

The Cognitive Area emphasizes such thought processes as understanding, remembering, problem solving, and creating. This area is subdivided into (1) knowledge and (2) intellectual skills and abilities.

Knowledge refers to recognition or recall of specific information, concepts, generalizations, and broad theories. Intellectual skills and abilities refer to the five ways of manipulating knowledge-comprehension, application, analysis, synthesis, and evaluation. Most educational objectives fall into the cognitive area, and most of the work in curriculum and test development deals with this area.

The *Psychomotor Area* emphasizes certain motor (muscular) skills, manipulation of various materials and objects, or certain acts that require neuromuscular coordination. These objectives are most often related to courses in handwriting, speech, and physical education, and to trade and technical courses.

The *Affective Area* emphasizes feeling, emotion, or a degree of acceptance or rejection. These objectives often are expressed as attitudes, appreciations, values, and emotional sets (biases). The learning related to these objectives is not so clearly understood as learning related to cognitive and psychomotor objectives.

Testing and evaluation

To determine the effectiveness of instruction, the performances of learners are evaluated by means of tests. In general, two types of tests are used: (1) tests of learning ability and (2) achievement tests. Tests of learning ability seek to measure the general ability that an individual can use to perform any task. Achievement tests are more specific, and most of them relate to particular scholastic or vocational areas.

A variety of instruments and procedures can be used to measure school achievement, including essay examinations, multiple-choice tests, and rating scales. An achievement test provides a single score indicating the student's relative achievement in a given field. A diagnostic test provides information on specific weaknesses, misunderstandings, or gaps in achievement.

Testing has become an accepted part of school practice. But questions have been raised about socioeconomic biases in intelligence testing. Educators and psychologists are attempting to develop culture-fair or culture-free intelligence tests that minimize the effects of environmental differences on test scores.

Educational Psychology is the use of psychological knowledge and psychological methods to solve educational problems. Educational psychologists organize information about learning and develop theories to explain people's behavior while learning.

They study the relationship of learning to a person's intelligence, interests, abilities, and motivation.

They develop techniques to study behavior and tests to measure different aspects of behavior.

They help to develop methods of teaching and studying, and investigate memory and methods of improving it.

Educational psychologists also evaluate the effectiveness of curriculums and of such teaching materials as television and teaching machines.

Educational psychologists work closely with schools. However, they are also interested in the education that takes place outside schools in the home and in recreational, social, and other group settings.

Much of the research that is conducted by educational psychologists concerns practical problems of education, even though these experts themselves may not deal directly with such problems. For example, they study the problems of social groups of students such as mentally retarded, deaf, or gifted children.

In addition, educational psychologists draw information from and contribute findings to many other areas of study within the field of psychology. These areas include emotion, learning, memory, motivation, personality, testing, abnormal psychology, developmental psychology, and social psychology.

To effectively study learning and teaching, educational psychologists must first consider the goals of education. Any statement of educational objectives includes a list of the things that students should be able to do after they have learned. Bloom's Taxonomy and Introduction: Literature and Critical Thinking provide more information in this area.

Bloom's Taxonomy is further explained in the following text:

Literature and Critical Thinking
BLOOMS TAXONOMY
THE BUILDING BLOCKS OF KNOWLEDGE

EVALUATION: JUDGING THE INFORMATION, STUDENT ASSESSES, RATES, VALUES, SELECTS "IF OUR POPULATION CONTINUES TO GROW, WHAT WILL THE U.S. BE LIKE IN 2020?"

SYNTHESIS: DOING SOMETHING NEW & DIFFERENT WITH INFORMATION, STUDENT HYPOTHESIZES, ABSTRACTS, CREATES, DESIGNS.

ANALYSIS: EXAMINING SPECIFIC PARTS OF THE INFORMATION. STUDENT CLASSIFIES, CATEGORIZES, COMPARES, ANALYZES, MAKES CAUSE & EFFECT RELATIONSHIPS. "COMPARE THE RESULTS OF THE FIRST, EXPERIMENT WITH RESULTS OF THE SECOND."

APPLICATION: USING THE INFORMATION. STUDENT CONSTRUCTS, INTERVIEWS, APPLIES, LISTS.

COMPREHENSION: UNDERSTANDING THE INFORMATION, STUDENT DEMONSTRATES, EXPLAINS, DESCRIBES, INTERPRETS, SUMMARIZES.

RECALL: LEARNING THE INFORMATION. REMEMBERING KNOWLEDGE, STUDENT RECALLS, RECITES, LISTS, LABELS, NAMES, REPEATS.

Chapter 2

Literature and Critical Thinking

IT IS POSSIBLE FOR ALL CHILDREN AT varying developmental levels to engage in a discovery process which clarifies thinking, increases knowledge, and deepens their understanding of human issues and social values. This activities book, based on Bloom's Taxonomy of Skills in the Cognitive Domain, provides teachers a resource to maximize this process, using distinguished children's literature as a vehicle.

The authors suggest the following options in using this book:

- OPTION 1: The teacher may select a single activity for the entire class.

- OPTION 2: The teacher may select different activities for single students or small groups of students.

- OPTION 3: The student may select the level at which he or she wishes to work once the teacher explains what is available.

The stories in this book follow the same format, so that each level of thinking skills is approached as follows.

Knowledge

This level provides the child with an opportunity to recall fundamental facts and information about the story. Success at this level will be evidenced by the child's ability to:

- Match character names with pictures of the characters.
- Identify the main characters in a crossword puzzle.
- Match statements with the characters who said them.
- List the main characteristics of one of the main characters in a WANTED poster.
- Arrange scrambled story pictures in sequential order.
- Arrange scrambled story sentences in sequential order.
- Recall details about the setting by creating a picture of where a part of the story took place.

Comprehension

This level provides the child with an opportunity to demonstrate a basic understanding of the story. Success at this level will be evidenced by the child's ability to:

- Interpret pictures of scenes from the story.
- Explain selected ideas or parts from the story in his or her own words.
- Draw a picture showing what happened before and after a passage or illustration found in the book.
- Write a sentence explaining what happened before and after a passage or illustration found in the book.
- Predict what could happen next in the story before the reading of the entire book is completed.
- Construct a pictorial time line which summarizes what happens in the story.

- Explain how the main character felt at the beginning, middle, and/or end of the story.

Application

This level provides the child with an opportunity to use information from the story in a new way. Success at this level will be evidenced by the child's ability to:

- Classify the characters as human, animal, or thing.

- Transfer a main character to a new setting.

- Make finger puppets and act out a part of the story.

- Select a meal that one of the main characters would enjoy eating, plan a menu, and a method of serving it.

- Think of a situation that occurred to a character in the story and write about how he or she would have handled the situation differently.

- Give examples of people the child knows who have the same problems as the characters in the story.

Analysis

This level provides the child with an opportunity to take parts of the story and examine these parts carefully in order to better understand the whole story. Success at this level will be evidenced by the child's ability to:

- Identify general characteristics (stated and/or implied) of the main characters.

- Distinguish what could happen from what couldn't happen in the story in real life.

- Select parts of the story that were funniest, saddest, happiest, and most unbelievable.

- Differentiate fact from opinion.

- Compare and/or contrast two of the main characters.

- Select an action of a main character that was exactly the same as something the child would have done.

Synthesis

This level provides the child with an opportunity to put parts from the story together in a new way to form a new idea or product. Success at this level will be evidenced by the child's ability to:

- Create a story from just the title before the story is read (pre-story exercise).

- Write three new titles for the story that would give a good idea of what it was about.

- Create a poster to advertise the story so people will want to read it.

- Create a new product related to the story.

- Restructure the roles of the main characters to create new outcomes in the story.

- Compose and perform a dialogue or monologue that will communicate the thoughts of the main character(s) at a given point in the story.

- Imagine that he or she is one of the main characters and write a diary account of daily thoughts and activities.

- Create an original character and tell how the character would fit into the story.

- Write the lyrics and music to a song that one of the main characters would sing if he/she became a rock star—and perform it.

Evaluation

This level provides the child with an opportunity to form and present an opinion backed up by sound reasoning. Success at this level will be evidenced by the child's ability to:

- Decide which character in the selection he or she would most like to spend a day with and why.

- Judge whether or not a character should have acted in a particular way and why.

- Decide if the story really could have happened and justify reasons for the decision.

- Consider how this story can help the child in his or her own life.

- Appraise the value of the story.

- Compare this story with another one the child has read.

- Write a recommendation as to why the books should be read or not.

In addition to the activities just outlined, a class project and a small group project will be included for each story.

How Children Learn

One of the most eminent child psychologists, Jerome Kagan, of Harvard University, has summarized succinctly what we know about how young children learn. According to him, the newborn is ready to experience most, if not all, of the basic sensations given our species from the moment of birth. The baby can see, hear, and smell and is sensitive to pain, touch, and changes in bodily position. Although the sensitivity of these modalities is not yet at its maximum ... the infant is responsive to information from all of the senses.

New knowledge is most often acquired when the infant's attention is focused on an event, and change is one of the central qualities governing the alertness and maintenance of the infant's attention. Particular changes in the pattern or arrangement of elements also have the ability to hold the infant's attention, at least during the first year of life.

Jean Piaget, a Swiss psychologist, made monumental contributions to our knowledge of how children learn to think. Piaget was not a professional psychologist but an epistemologist, interested in the study of the mechanisms by which children acquire bodies of knowledge. He closely observed children of different ages, starting with early infancy.

Piaget devised simple but ingenious experiments, such as showing children of different ages two similar glasses filled with water, pouring the water from one glass into a tall, thin glass, and asking the child which glass had more water in it. Or he asked questions, such as, "What makes the clouds move?" From their answers, he traced the evolution of children's concepts of the world and the objects in them into an accurate image of the world.

He hypothesized that the child's actions are the raw materials out of which knowledge and thought are generated. He further postulated a motivational force that impels the child to integrate and organize more and more complex stimuli into his level of cognition, allowing him to grasp and comprehend more and more about the world around him.

Piaget, like all creative thinkers, made bold leaps in his concepts and formulations, not all of which have stood the test of time. But he made a tremendous contribution to our understanding of the mind of the child and how it matures.

Piaget's cognitive theories explain intellectual development. They help us understand the individual structures and thinking processes of thought as well as the internal needs for new thoughts. This understanding of the thought process that has come from cognitive theories has been applied almost exclusively to theories of education.

Where education used to involve teaching students such concepts as match through lectures or demonstrations, it now appears that teaching new concepts is much easier to do if children can have hands-on experience with objects that they can manipulate. In this way, they can develop abstract possibilities and solutions using specific concrete activities.

On the other hand, this discussion would lead one to believe that cognitive growth will occur regardless of the individual's place in the culture or society. According to Piaget, the emphasis on development is in the way a child thinks and on the child's interactions with the surrounding inanimate and animate world. Because Piaget sees children as active in their environment, the concept of knowledge acquisition is not a static event. It is a lifetime developmental process and affects the ways of acquiring knowledge and change as children react and interact differently with the environment and with the world. It is as though Piaget equates knowledge acquisition and development as the same sort of process.

Piaget's theory is a stage theory; each stage builds upon the information attained by the previous stage. Each stage builds on what came before and provides a basis for what will follow.

Certain basic assumptions underlie Piaget's cognitive theory. First, in order for a child to attain all of the stages listed, the child must experience normal, healthy, biological cognitive growth. Any child who is in one way or another impaired intellectually may develop slower, or not reach one of the higher stages, or not attain many of the concepts within a given stage. Therefore, the individual stages coincide with development of the brain.

The second assumption is that, all things being equal, an individual will indeed go through all of these stages following biological growth of the brain, provided the environment allows sufficient experiences to help in practice with the newly developed abilities of each new stage.

The third assumption is that there is a homeostatic mechanism that promotes cognitive changes. This is the mechanism of "equilibrium." Essentially, every individual wants to maintain a sense of cognitive balance or organization. When new information is presented or biological growth causes a new thinking process to be available, a period of disequilibrium is presented. This happens because the new information is presented or biological growth causes a new thinking process to be available; therefore, a period of disequilibrium is presented. This happens because the new information or process confronts our organization.

In order to regain equilibrium, our thinking must be changed to either include the information or adopt new thinking principles. This involves old "schemas" or constructing new ones. Schemas are mental concepts which guide or influence interaction with the environment.

For example, an infant's first schema with regard to its parent might be that crying causes an adult to come. However, as the child develops language capabilities, that schema may be broadened to include not only crying but also yelling, "Mommy" or "Daddy" and having an adult come. With advanced development and advanced language capabilities, the child's schema about how to get an adult to meet its needs expands to include language as well as other possible behaviors.

When new situations or information cause disequilibrium, a process of adaption helps return the individual to a state of equilibrium. Adaptation involves bringing the new information from the world or about the world into the schema and either incorporating that into the existing schema or changing the schema. The process of bringing information in and letting the current schema handle it is a process known as *assimilation*.

With the above example, a child learns that crying will also bring an adult, that is, a variant on the form of crying. However, with new biological processes ongoing in the brain and the ability of the infant now to use language, the infant learns that something entirely different or qualitatively different from a scream can also bring about the presence of an adult. This changing of a schema is a process known as *accommodation*.

In essence, then, people achieve balance through adaptation of schemas that are used to deal with the world. Either the schema can handle new information and processes with a slight expansion (assimilation), or the schema must change (accommodation). Generally speaking, if the process changes, it results in new schemas.

Lastly, all organisms actively seek knowledge and stimulation. Therefore, cognitive development will occur as individuals handle all new forms of information. This can be seen simply with *habituation*, a process whereby something is continually presented to an infant until it is no longer of interest to the infant.

According to Piaget, it is no longer of any interest because there is no new knowledge in the presentations, and therefore, no other cognitive development can occur.

Piaget formulated a systematic model to explain how the child goes successively from one stage or level of cognitive ability to another as he or she grows older. In organizing the data he obtained from children, Piaget was critical of the one-sided approach that viewed the child as a passive organism whose mind was shaped by his or her cumulative life experiences.

He also rejected the notion that the infant was endowed with an innate intellectual capacity that unfolded and matured with age. Rather, he conceived intelligence as the outcome of the child's adaptation to the world in successive stages, which he considered to have an invariant sequence. It was the child's action on the environment, starting with the innate ability to respond to the sensory and motor stimuli with which he or she is born. That, Piaget considered crucial to his or her intellectual development.

Piaget called the first stage *sensorimotor intelligence*, encompassing the infancy period (up to 2 years). In his formulation, the neonate begins life with a set of motor and sensory reflexes that are the foundation for his or her interaction with the environment. Out of this interaction, the infant learns to coordinate the sensory and motor experiences into an awareness of the external world as a permanent place with objects that are independent of his or her own perceptions.

As one example, the neonate starts with a grasping reflex, which is elicited by stimulating the palm of his or her hand. As he or she grasps various objects, the infant learns to experience different shapes, textures, weights, and temperatures.

The second stage in Piaget's system is the period of *preoperational representation*, which extends approximately from age 2 to age 7. In this stage, the child internalizes his or her sensorimotor experiences and their imprints in the brain in symbolic representations. Language development during this period is one example of this symbolic transformation. Words become symbols of objects, people, categories, and activities.

In the next stage, that of concrete operations extending from age 7 to age 12, the child begins to structure and integrate his or her thoughts into a coherent system to make classifications of objects and their properties and to abstract concepts such as length, width, volume, and time. These mental operations are applied to concrete objects, known by the term *concrete operations* for this stage.

Finally, after age 12, the child becomes capable of formal operations, which Piaget viewed as the most advanced form of cognitive activity. Some people may not reach this stage. In this style of formal operations, the child or adult is no longer bound by concrete objects and relationships but is able to grasp abstract concepts, potential realities, and the implications of various assumptions and ideas.

Piaget's work has had an enormous influence on thinking and research in cognitive psychology. His basic formulations have been the basis of innumerable studies that have been applied fruitfully to different groups of children and adolescents under various experimental and natural situations.

Many studies have indicated that children do not necessarily move smoothly from one stage to another in the way Piaget thought. Children, and even adults, can perform some tasks at a higher level of development and other tasks only at a lower level. This has become so evident that psychologists have begun to question the notion of a period or a stage, and some have abandoned the notion.

Furthermore, Piaget concentrated his studies on the development of logical thinking and ignored such issues as fantasy, the role of special talents, and the role of emotion and motivation in relation to thought. Also, Piaget developed an abstract theoretical scheme to describe how the child absorbs and integrates new experiences, a scheme which depends on concepts such as "schemas," "assimilation," and "accommodation," that are so general and vague that they have been of little use as guidelines to other researchers.

But with all these limitations, Piaget has remained a pioneer in opening up systematic and objective methods of tracing the development of thought in children. Without the stimulus that his work and ideas provided, the advances in cognitive psychology would have come much more slowly and painfully.

Classifying Teaching Methods

Educational psychologists and other researchers examine teaching methods from one of three points of view—sociological, administrative, or psychological.

From a *sociological viewpoint*, the social, emotional, and cultural background of teachers and students are examined. Student backgrounds and conditions under which a class is being taught are considered the most important factors in determining patterns of teaching behavior. From this viewpoint, researchers might study how to teach culturally deprived children or children at risk.

The *administrative point of view* considers how to teach large numbers of students who differ in ability and needs. Two administrative approaches to this problem are ungraded schools and team teaching.

The *psychological point of view* is concerned with the creation of standardized tests, which is a highly specialized area in educational psychology. In achievement testing, the custom is to analyze a course into a list of the elements of the course content. The psychologist must also specify the objectives in terms of expected behaviors and levels of performance.

Group data are used to evaluate a teaching method or a curriculum. Comparisons of groups of students are made to determine whether performance is better under one set of conditions than under another. These results provide the basis for making decisions about what to teach and how to teach.

Teaching methods

Most programs of instruction are developed to encourage students to achieve specific course objectives. In an ungraded school, students are grouped according to such factors as age and ability, rather than grade level. Students progress at their own speed through material to be learned. Team teaching eliminates having one teacher for each grade or for each classroom. Instead, a team of specialists in various subjects instructs a group of students.

From a psychological point of view, teaching methods are defined in terms of what teachers do when teaching. A researcher might study how a teacher uses rewards and punishments in learning situations. Teaching methods designed from a psychological viewpoint consider a student's psychological requirements as well as the student's needs for knowledge and skills.

For example, teaching machines individualize learning by letting students proceed at their own rate. Some were studies of the role of the teacher, and others were studies of conditions in the classroom. Few studies measured learning itself. Also, conditions varied from one teacher to another, even though both teachers were supposedly using the same method. Therefore, the hundreds of studies of group methods really examined only a few different methods.

Studies of group methods were also unsatisfactory because the results varied and seldom showed that one technique was better than another.

For example, some studies show that permissive, or nondirective, teaching is better than authoritarian, or directive, teaching. But an almost equal number of studies indicate the opposite. Comparison of the project method of teaching with the subject-matter method of teaching has also produced inconclusive results.

Computer-assisted instruction is a method of teaching in which a computer makes decisions about the course of instruction to be given a student. Some computer-based systems use a form of programmed instruction called *idiographic programming*. In idiographic programming, a student's performance on tests and on other sections of the program help determine both what the student is taught and the way the student tests.

Chapter 3

A Comparsion of Theories of Child Development in the Twentieth Century

COGNITIVE THEORIES LOOK AT DEVELOPMENT from the viewpoint of how an individual processes information from the environment. According to Piaget, we begin life as basically a set of reflexes but quickly advance through a series of changes in our ability to think. As these abilities change, our perception of the world changes, and subsequently, we change.

Learning theory takes a viewpoint that stresses the responses of individuals to daily events and how the consequences of those responses may change our expectations of future events. Whereas the previous stage theories look at development from a very broad view, learning theory allows us to see the developmental process and its resultant changes from the viewpoint of the effects of individual events.

Most developmental psychologists tend to endorse an eclectic theoretical stance. Basically, they use the parts of each theory that may explain a current situation best. Thus, the process of development can be seen as being explained by the combination of a number of different theories.

The enormous growth of scientific research and activity since World War II has included psychology as one of the recognized life sciences. Psychology now makes no small contribution to the rapid change in Western culture and civilization, a contribution that consists of a stream of new discoveries. Psychology also makes a contribution to its own maintenance. That lies in teaching, for every academic generation must train the next. The roots of psychology must grow if the branches are to spread and the seeds of new growth germinate in the classroom.

Children are active constructors of their own learning. There has been great interest in recent years in children as cognitive beings. Children can selectively attend to different aspects of their environments: seeing, searching, remembering, monitoring, correcting, validating, and problem-solving activities, which build cognitive competencies.

A wave of experimental challenges to Piagetian formulations has not reduced our interest in cognitive development. On the contrary, there has been a heightened interest in preschool learners changing over time. Because of what we know about oral language competencies, Cashdan summarized this model well.

There are two ways in which we can help a child learn. One of them is by attempting to teach him; the other is by facilitating his attempts to teach himself. We need to give the child freedom to explore and to learn on his own. The child is self-stimulating and self-starting, provided conditions are right for him.

It now appears as though it is not enough to only give the child freedom to explore and learn on his own, although this remains very important. We must not crowd out his scope for doing such learning, but we must consider some further evidence. There are three bodies of recent knowledge about children's learning which we must consider. These are:

1. Research on child behaviors which shows that the child is affected by what immediately follows what he had done, that is, what is contingent on behavior.

2. Research about the importance of contexts which tell that children select what they attend to, shape their own learning environments to some extent, and evoke responses from those environments in consistent ways.

3. Research on parent-child and teacher-child interactions.

When we interact with children who are learning, we take the context into account and we respond to what we think are the constructions being built up in their minds. As part of the teacher's careful observation, he or she attends more contingently and responds more appropriately. The teacher provides temporary support systems which help the child to function effectively and can lead to the child taking over independent action before long.

These new sources of information are important because it is now possible to argue how some styles of teaching may facilitate the development of independent, constructive learners and some styles of teaching may either confuse the learners or impede progress toward independence.

Important changes take place in the character of learning at the end of the preschool years.

- The older child plans more than the younger does.
- The older child's learning is often mediated by words, whereas that of the younger child is less often mediated.
- The older child can deal with several features at a time and in some structured relationships, while the younger child tends to manage one aspect at a time and depends on the properties he can perceive rather than those he knows about.
- The younger child operates on items in their contexts, while the older child depends less on contextual settings and is able to bring together experiences from several settings.

By 5 years, the child begins more actively to organize and relate his information about the world-coding, categorizing, sorting, and applying learned coding systems to new events. He depends less on the association of things that have occurred together or on responses that have produced contingent results. He tries to solve an incongruity, direct his thinking to some past event, organize his experiences in related categories, label things, recall verbally things he has observed, and draw on things that he has heard about. He has been doing all these things in some sense since he was an infant, but now he does more of these things deliberately.

This has been described in relation to some research on memory. At 3 to 4 years, the child cannot yet set himself a goal to memorize or to recall. Memorizing, like recalling, is accomplished unintentionally at this age. The 3- to 4-year-old children mainly memorize and recall connections formed by constantly repeating the spatial and temporal contiguity of impinging objects and phenomena.

A young child does well in memorizing connected text, like nursery rhymes, stories, and fairy tales. In this case, along with a number of repetitions, a number of conditions are present that favor memorizing such as:

- Emotional content of the text
- Clear images
- Evocation of empathy
- Rhythm of speech and rhythm of body movement which facilitate the construction of a verbal-motor image
- Memorable play on words

Before 5 years, we see the appearance and gradual development of intentional memorizing and recalling. Then we can note the single intentional repetition of material that must be kept in memory, and by 6 or 7 years, the child, with improved efficiency, is able to:

- Analyze the material to be remembered
- Group it
- Establish logical connections, and
- Systematize representations of the surrounding environment

Experimental evidence suggests that the memory is more than a copying device. It uses what it already knows to reconstruct the material that it is supposed to remember.

The 5- to 7-year age group is a particularly interesting one for cognitive development. Piaget has described this as a period of transition from perceptual learning to the thinking operations of the child who can classify and consider inverse relationships. Writers like Margaret Donaldson have emphasized that the effects of environment and instructions are greater than Piaget allowed and that this may allow for a powerful teaching environment to accelerate development in limited areas.

Russian child psychologists like vygotsky and his colleagues have described a transition from self-instructions, spoken aloud, to inner self-instructions, in the 5- to 7-year period.

Experimental studies of children's learning have suggested some interesting transitions taking place at this time which speed up the process of acquiring new skills or reapplying old ones. (For example, the child can produce a whole new set of behaviors merely by applying the concept of "opposite" to old learning.) It is a period when the child learns strategies, or ways, of proceeding which help him to find his own way around new learning. He learns a great deal more about how to instruct himself.

Chapter 4

The Middle Twentieth-Century Theories of Childhood: An Introduction To Dewey, Montessori, Erikson, Piaget and Vygotsky

Dewey's Theory

Dewey is most associated with the progressive education movement in America. He played a central role in its development in the United States. During this period in history, Maria Montessori and Jean Piaget were spreading the same messages in Europe. These early theorists agreed that all children learn from doing and that education should involve real-life material and experiences. They also believed that education should encourage experimentation and independent thinking.

As a progressive educator, Dewey shared with vygotsky, Montessori, and Piaget the central ideas of that movement: education should be child-centered; education must be both active and interactive; and education must involve the social world of the child and the community.

Montessori's Theories

Montessori's theories about children have influenced the way all early childhood programs are structured today. Her work provided a foundation for the work of Piaget and vygotsky. Many of the ideas held by people who work in early childhood education today can be traced to Montessori.

Erikson's Theory

Erikson's theory, which is called the Eight Ages of Man, covers the entire life span of a human being. It is Erikson's idea that each stage of development has a task that must be accomplished. Successful resolution of each stage affects the next stage. As people pass through each stage, they form personality strengths or weaknesses based on their development during that stage. Describing this, Erikson gave us the term identity crisis.

Piaget's Theory

Piaget thought that neither position explains learning by itself, but that the child's interactions with his environment are what create learning. He claimed that children construct their own knowledge by giving meaning to the people, places, and things in their world.

Vygotsky's Theory

Vygotsky has changed the way educators think about children's interactions with others. His work showed that social and cognitive development work together and build on each other. For years, early educators, schooled in Piaget's theories, viewed children's knowledge as being constructed from personal experiences. Although vygotsky also believed this, he thought that personal and social experience cannot be separated. The world children inhabit is shaped by their families, communities, socioeconomic status, education, and culture.

Chapter 5

A Comparison of Studies in Behavior Modification and Piaget's Theory of Cognitive Development

For the Challenge of the Twenty-First Century

This book is a major contribution to educational psychology. It is a unique combination of sound theory and insightful application and should be required reading for every professional. It is one of the most exciting books written in educational and developmental psychology in the twenty-first century. It also includes a unique contribution to multicultural education, particularly for teachers and those who prepare teachers to understand that individual differences in cognitive development may be influenced by family, culture, personality, and socialization of the two sexes.

The nature of human learning

There is no complete agreement among scientists and educators on the nature of human learning. But certain ideas are generally accepted. Learning theories are based largely on findings of modern psychology. Most theories of learning can be divided into three main groups: (1) behavior modification theories; (2) cognitive theories; and (3) humanistic theories. All three groups attempt to explain how students can best achieve the goals of education. Each group stresses a different kind of learning and recommends different methods of achieving it. Most educators make use of all three types of theories, and most students probably learn in all three ways.

Behavior modification or stimulus-response theories

Behavior modification theories state that learning consists of forming habits. The habits may be mental habits, such as knowing that 2+2=4 or that some actions are considered "good" and others "bad." Or the habits may be partly physical, such as knowing how to throw a ball or pound a nail.

According to behavior modification theories, a person does not form a habit unless it is rewarding or satisfying to him. For example, a child might learn that 2+2=4 only if a parent or teacher praises him when he gives the right answer but withholds praise when he gives the wrong one. Using a series of simple habits as stepping-stones, a student can gradually be led to form more complicated habits, such as operating complex machinery or solving difficult mathematical problems.

Behavior modification theories work best with problems that have one solution. To find out whether a student has learned the solution, a teacher should be able to observe the results. Behavior modification theories, therefore, stress types of learning where results can be measured or tested. Such learning includes the acquiring of factual knowledge and such skills as the ability to solve mathematical problems or speak a foreign language.

Cognitive, or problem-solving theories

Cognitive theories stress the importance of thought processes in learning. Such processes include understanding relationships between things and deciding which solution to a problem is the best one. Those who support this type of theory believe that behavior modification theories cannot explain or help develop the most complex thought processes. They also believe that many problems have more than one correct solution.

Cognitive theories, therefore, propose a method of learning called the *discovery method*. In this method, a teacher helps a student select a problem to solve. The teacher guides the student to the necessary materials and information and asks questions that encourage the student to think. But each student is expected to work out his own solution to the problem.

Humanistic theories

Humanistic theories stress the importance of the emotions in learning. Supporters of this type of theory believe that behavior modification and cognitive theories neglect a student's emotional development. Humanistic theories point out that every individual has a personality different from that of all other persons. As a result, each student should be allowed to develop in his own way.

Humanistic theories consider emotional development important both in itself and as an aid to all other types of learning. According to humanistic theory, a teacher should help a student examine his emotional needs and desires and encourage him to acquire the knowledge and skills needed to fulfill them.

How Teachers Guide Learning

The teacher's main task is to create conditions that will encourage and stimulate learning. Teachers must help students develop their own initiative and ability to think critically. Good teachers guide students in seeking important knowledge and analyzing possible solutions to meaningful problems. They also help students understand important values involved in dealing with various problems. Teachers use a variety of methods to achieve the desired learning goals. They also use such teaching aids as books, audio-visual materials, teaching machines, and field trips.

Good teachers are well educated, know their subject, and understand their students. They are familiar with the principles of education, the psychology of human development, and the theories of learning.

Theories of teaching have not been as fully developed as have theories of learning. Many educators feel that a theory of learning also provides sufficient guidelines for teaching. Most teachers probably use a combination of behavior modification, cognitive, and humanistic teaching principles. Many teachers do not consciously follow any theory, but rather depend on experience and intuition to guide them.

The Role of Parents

Mothers and fathers can best promote the development of their children in three major ways. They can do so by (1) understanding a child's basic needs, (2) motivating the child's behavior, and (3) serving as models of appropriate behaviors.

All children have certain basic physical and psychological needs. Both sets of needs must be met if a child is to develop normally. Poor physical health may harm a child's psychological development, and psychological problems may affect a child physically.

Children need regular, nourishing meals, proper clothing, and a clean, comfortable home. They also require a reasonable amount of play and exercise and enough space to play in.

Basic psychological skills and needs of children are determined by the skills and personality that a child develops in his or her home and should be encouraged in every society. All children, therefore, have certain basic psychological needs.

Toddlers, for example, need to develop self-confidence, and so they must feel loved, wanted, and respected. Toddlers should also have enough sufficient variety in their routine to help them develop language skills. Preschoolers especially need close contact with adults they like and admire. Such contacts help promote normal emotional development.

Parents motivate a child when they encourage the child to adopt a certain type of behavior. The mobile infant, his family members, and his caregiver are entering a stage of development that is laced with complicated feelings about separation and attachment, much excitement, and many challenges. At one moment, the baby is consumed with his own movement—crawling, scooting, or toddling off. In the next minute, he is fighting to keep the adult close, crying if left for a moment.

Each partner in the triangle of relationships may experience different feelings at different times; thus, honest communication between parent and caregiver takes on added importance. Working together, they can keep their focus on what is most important for the infant. They can identify and experiment with ways to maintain his sense of security in the childcare setting, reinforcing daily his understanding that his parents will be back, that they still love him, and that his caregiver will love and protect him while his family is away.

As with young infants, open and frequent communication is needed to assure continuity between family and caregiver. Parents and caregivers of mobile infants must keep pace with their rapid development by changing the environment and making decisions about how to encourage mobility independence and curiosity within safe boundaries.

Negotiations with families must be guided by the caregiver's commitment to reaching a mutual understanding. For example, a mutual understanding of the use of "no" as a statement of independence is needed. Many families do not believe that it is appropriate to allow a young child to say "no." In some cultures, such statements of independence, especially when directed toward an adult, are viewed as highly inappropriate. Cultural beliefs and rules about infants self-feeding, being "loud," and moving without restraint also vary.

Behavior Modification in the Classroom

Because research evidence indicates the value to children of receiving approval from their teachers, as well as the generally unequal distribution of that approval, efforts have been made to reward children more methodically and, thereby, modify their behavior. Although teaching itself is in many ways an art, one that cannot be taught, children's behavior in the classroom can be improved by behavior modification techniques.

In a typical behavior modification treatment, baseline observations are first made, class periods are broken down into brief intervals, and a record is kept of the percent of intervals in which children behave as desired. The teacher then increases the frequency of his or her positive comments to students for appropriate behavior, and then observations are made of the effects on children's classroom behavior.

To check that the manipulation is really responsible for greater frequency of desired behavior, the teacher may discontinue systematic reinforcement and see whether good behavior returns to the baseline frequency. She or he then increases reinforcement once more, and this time, continues it. Periodic checks ensure that the desired behavior is still being reinforced and that the children are still behaving well.

This kind of treatment has been used effectively in many classrooms to increase decorum. Many teachers use contingent rewards: if the students are quiet, their recess or playtime is increased. Deals and contracts are made between children and parents, whereby parents promise a suitable reward such as a video game if children's behavior improves.

Rewards have been effective. Daily report cards, which determine whether children gain or lose home privileges, have also worked. Systems in which children earn points and tokens that can be exchanged for candy, money, toys, and privileges have decreased disruptive behaviors, even when other methods—rules, praise, ignoring disruptions—have had little effect.

As James Sherman and Don Bushell point out, however, token systems have a problem: when tokens are no longer given, improvements in behavior disappear. It seems that decorum bought by tokens does not generalize to other situations and is not itself maintained unless the special token system is kept in place. Sherman and Bushell suggest that reinforcements be built into the classroom program and that more research be done on training students to respond to long-term consequences, rather than immediate rewards.

Piaget's Theory of Cognitive Development

While others of his time argued that learning is either intrinsic (coming from the child) or extrinsic (imposed by the environment or taught by adults), Piaget thought that neither position explains learning by itself, but that the child's interactions with his environment are what create learning. He claimed that children construct their own knowledge by giving meaning to the people, places, and things in their world.

Piaget was fond of the expression "construction is superior to instruction" (Joanne Hendrick, *The Whole Child*, Englewood Cliffs, N.J. Merril, 1992). By this, he meant that children learn best when they are actually doing the work themselves and creating their own understanding of what's going on, instead of being given explanations by adults.

He was a student of Montessori's work and built on her idea that meaningful work was important to children's cognitive development. Like Montessori, Piaget believed children needed every possible opportunity to do things for themselves. For example, children might be interested in how things grow. If a teacher reads them an illustrated book on how things grow, this instruction will increase the child's knowledge base. But if the child has the opportunity to actually plant a garden at school, the process of digging, watering, observing, and actually experiencing growing things will help the child to construct a knowledge of growing things that he cannot ever achieve merely by looking at a picture.

Like Dewey, Piaget believed that children learn only when their curiosity is not fully satisfied. He thought that children's curiosity actually drives their learning. According to Piaget, the best strategy for preschool curriculum is to keep children curious, make them wonder, and offer them real problem-solving challenges, rather than giving them information.

Many adults still hold the notion that a teacher is someone who shares information. Using Piaget's theory about children's learning requires changing the image of the teacher into someone who nurtures inquiry and supports the child's own search for answers.

Piaget also stressed the importance of play as an important avenue for learning. As children engage in symbolic play (making a cake out of sand, using a garden hose to be a firefighter), they make sense of the object and activities that surround them. As they imitate what goes on around them, they begin to understand how things work and what things are for. Initially this is a process of trial and error. However, with time and repetition, children use new information to increase their understanding of the world around them.

Piaget believed that all children pass through the same stages when developing their thinking skills. The age at which children accomplish these stages of development can vary. Because of this variation, charts outlining Piaget's stages may also differ slightly.

Parents and teachers should always remember that individual children have their own rates of development. Differences in development stretch over a broad continuum. For example, many books cite 10 to 13 months as a typical age range for first steps. Yet, some children walk as early as 8 months and others as late as 18 months.

Many teachers and other adults wonder if there are things that prevent growth or if there are ways to hurry development along. Piaget believed that children's intellectual growth is based partly on physical development. He also believed that it is affected by children's interactions with the environment. He did not believe that teachers can "teach" young children to understand a concept. He was certain that children build their own understanding of the world by the things they do.

According to Piaget, children's cognitive development passes through various stages. The following chapter is a basic discussion of Piaget's stages in children's journey to build knowledge. The first two stages are the stages that most concern teachers in early care and education settings.

Humanistic Theories: Maslow and Rogers

Another approach to personality theory is humanistic. Scholars who advance the humanistic view see individuals as all-important entities, endowed with the potential to be self-directed and responsible for their own destiny.

Maslow and Rogers are two leading humanistic psychologists. Both believe that everybody has a drive toward self-actualization, which is the ultimate motivating force for all ages. Both take the position that whatever has happened to a person in the past, no matter how unfortunate, need not necessarily spell doom to later efforts to realize potentialities. They hold that past experiences are important only to the extent that they directly influence today. People's current situation depends even more on what they seek for themselves in the future.

Maslow believes that attainment of the ultimate step in personality development—self-actualization—is unlikely unless other basic needs are satisfied first. Food and water are primary necessities. Next come safety and security. After that, one needs love and affection. Self-esteem is the next prerequisite. Only if all those needs are met, according to Maslow, can self-actualization be achieved.

Rogers has a slightly different approach. He holds that everybody has an overwhelming, biologically based drive to realize his or her own potential. This drive transcends everything else. According to Rogers, self-actualization is a biological fact for all living things. Unlike Maslow, Rogers holds that there are no indispensable prerequisites. For example, a woman who is a good mother realizes an important physiological potential. So there are no insurmountable barriers to self-actualization. All one needs to do is to keep one's eye on the future.

People want to feel good about themselves, to increase self-regard, according to Rogers. In some cases, the approval of an audience is necessary. But the pleasure of self-actualization can also be realized all alone: by shooting a dozen baskets in solitary practice, writing a poem, even cleaning a house till it shines. Someone with a strong drive toward fulfillment can overcome past problems by concentrating on the goal.

Maslow, Rogers, Erikson, and Freud proposed personality theories that have many similarities as well as differences. One common thread is the importance of heredity and early parental influence in shaping the development of any individual's personality.

Jean Piaget is probably the major theorist on the whole question of cognitive development. Many compare his importance in the field of child development to Freud's in psychiatry. Major contributions to the theory of cognitive development have also been made by others, notably Jerome Bruner and Jerome Kagan, both of whom have done major work with children in university workshops in this country.

According to Piaget's theory, developed by observing children at various ages, the way human beings think progresses through four major periods: (a) sensorimotor activities, from birth to 2 years; (b) preoperational thought, from 2 to 7 years; (c) concrete operational thought, from 7 to 11 years; and (d) formal operational thought, from 11 to 15 years.

His progression brings a body from an initial inability to differentiate between itself and its surroundings, to the next period, in which the world and self are seen as separate, although the child cannot yet think either abstractly or in relative terms. In the third period, a youngster can understand symbols and deal with different dimensions of a problem or a situation all at once. Finally, as adulthood approaches, a young person is able to be logical and to think out a problem deductively.

Bruner's theory of cognitive growth is somewhat similar to Piaget's, but the stages Bruner describes and what they emphasize are different. According to Bruner, a child moves through three stages of cognitive development: (a) enactive, characterized by activity (this corresponds to Piaget's sensorimotor period); (b) iconic, dominated by imagery and visual perceptions (this corresponds to Piaget's preoperational period); and (c) symbolic, which involves the use of symbols, such as words or mathematical formulas (this corresponds to Piaget's concrete operational period). Thus, the child's cognitive growth moves from motor activity, to pictorial representations, and finally to symbolic representations.

The theories of Piaget and Bruner help parents and teachers to understand how children think at various ages and stages, enabling them to make sense out of children's "bright sayings" and "foolish" errors.

In Piaget's theory, a 4-year-old child is shown two identical glasses of water, side by side. Each glass contains the same amount of liquid at the same level. The child is asked to describe the glasses and their contents, and the child readily reports that the two are alike.

Then, with the youngster watching, water is poured from one of the glasses into another glass, taller and narrower than the original. The water level, of course, has become higher. When the child is asked, "Does one have more water than the other?"

The answer will be that the taller, narrower glass has more. Why? Because the water is "higher"!

Then, if the water in the third, taller glass is put back into the original glass, the child will have a change of mind. Now the young observer will say the water in the two original glasses is again the same.

This classic experiment with water glasses, which was devised by Piaget, reveals an important characteristic in the early development of thinking: *egocentrism*. Children of preschool age are characteristically egocentric. They perceive information or a situation from only one point of view—their own—and they perceive only one aspect of a situation at a time. (Egocentrism in this context does not mean that the child is selfish, only unable to transcend limited cognitive ability.) Egocentric children pay attention only to the level of water in the containers. Their thinking cannot yet take into account the additional aspect of the diameter of the containers. They are not disturbed by their own obvious (to an adult) illogic. Their thinking is irreversible—they do not mentally return the water to the original glass (after it has made its appearance in the taller, narrower one). Nor do they realize that the initial amount is still present. They focus only on the present water levels.

Young children's irreversibility is demonstrated by their inability to understand operations or reversible events. Operations are events that have an end point but that can be returned to the starting point. For example, 2+2=4; 4-2=2. The water level experiment is another example of a reversible event.

Now, if a 7-year-old is subjected to the same water level operation, the response will be quite different. The older child agrees that the water in the first two glasses is the same. But the youngster also realizes that the same liquid poured into a differently shaped glass continues to have the same volume as before. The child has, in fact, grown into a higher stage of thinking ability and has progressed from egocentrism to increasing relativism.

At this point, the youngster begins to decenter—to perceive information or a situation from more than one point of view. The child has achieved the ability to think reversibility: the young mind is able to "put the water back" into the original glass and to conclude that it is still the same amount of water.

Is there any practical reason for a parent or teacher to bother with this wardrobe of terms and descriptions? None at all. But it is important to understand the principles behind the terms if a conscientious caregiver would like to be able to communicate effectively with a child. How many adults have been exasperated by preschoolers' squabbles about who has "more" juice when the glasses just happen to be different sizes and shapes? The children are not being ornery. They think they are seeing a real injustice.

What is going on inside children's minds as they develop from egocentric to relativistic thought? Piaget conceives the thought process as being composed of a kind of building block, which he calls a scheme.

Schemes are the fundamental units of thought and action. They are mental formulas about how the world works, which can be generalized or changed from one situation to another. For example, a baby forms a mental image—a scheme—of Mother and Father. This is the formula that makes it possible to distinguish friend from possible foe. When a baby's face is frowned up at the sight of a stranger and the child begins to cry, the event may be proof that thought is going on about who is who, based on clear schemes of those who are familiar.

A baby's sucking reflex is an early scheme. Later, it can be generalized or applied to other objects—sucking fingers, nipples, and rattles. Schemas may also interact with one another and become organized or combined into acts. Example: when an infant sucks (a scheme) at the sight of a nipple (another scheme), two schemes are being organized.

The key to cognitive growth, according to Piaget, is the process he terms *equilibration*. Equilibration is the tendency to function at a more complex level, to move from one developmental stage to the next. When schemes are organized to produce new, more complicated behavior, equilibration is said to have taken place. Thus, a baby progresses from sucking to drinking from a cup. Or an infant tires of a simple toy and looks for another with more challenge.

Even the handling of the same rattle can illustrate equilibration. First, a baby looks at it, then puts it in its mouth, later shakes it, and then throws it out of the crib. Confronted with new objects or events in the course of daily experience, the child tries to incorporate them into its repertoire of schemes. The result is equilibration—the organization of schemes into more complex behavior in order to meet new situations.

In organizing schemes as a response to new experiences, adaptation is taking place. *Adaptation* is the reaction to new experiences through assimilation and accommodation. *Assimilation* is adding new information into one's frame of knowledge, or schemes. *Accommodation* is changing one's frame of knowledge to include new information that cannot be assimilated. Accommodation takes place when the new information does not fit into the "old" picture.

For instance, a child sucks a rattle like a nipple. Or an older child who is familiar with the color blue calls a purple dress "blue." In these cases, assimilation has taken place. But accommodation occurs when the baby realizes that a rattle will yield no nourishment and the child learns that blue and purple are, in fact, two different colors. In both instances, old schemes have been modified to fit new situations and a new state of equilibration has been achieved.

Another example: a baby picks up a pen and sucks on it. That's assimilation. The child has applied an already-acquired scheme (sucking) to a new "event" (pen). Then the baby notices that the pen made marks on the playpen pad and makes some more marks on purpose. That's accommodation. The child has modified its behavior to include the new experience. The two processes add up to equilibration—they progress from one developmental stage to the next. Thus do maturation and an increasing number of experiences result in continuous adjustment and development and more appropriate responses to the environment.

Many examples of assimilation and accommodation can be found in adult thought processes. Confronted with the task of learning a new language, most of us resist and try merely to assimilate. We seek resemblances between the new language and the one we already know. But we soon learn that we must accept a new kind of grammar and new rules of pronunciation; we accommodate.

Inappropriate assimilation is an act of egocentrism. (It is ego-centric to apply the rules of our own language to another tongue.) Accommodation takes place when assimilation fails and some sort of adjustment to the new objects or events is necessary. (We learn the rules of the foreign language.) A child or an adult changes what is already known in order to deal with a new experience.

Another example from a child's world: a child who has a dog may, when first introduced to a cat, call it a "doggie." After being told it is a cat, the youngster has a change of mind, modifies the previous scheme the child is learning and accommodating.

Psychologists see thinking as a process that keeps changing in one way or another throughout life. However, Piaget's theory traces cognitive development only from birth through adolescence, the age span that he actually observed and described in detail. His principles are illustrated by what happens in the various stages of mental development.

According to Piaget, as we have seen, cognitive behavior develops through four major periods: (a) sensorimotor activities from birth to approximately 2 years; (b) preoperational thought from about 2 to about 7 years; (c) concrete operational thought from around 7 to approximately 11 years; and (d) formal operational thought from roughly 11 to 15 years.

It is important to note that Piaget's norms are not accepted by all psychologists. Many investigators believe that young children are really more advanced than Piaget gives them credit. Another contention is that formal reasoning only begins to emerge between the ages of 11 and 15 and that not all formal reasoning tasks can be dealt with by age 15.

During the sensorimotor period, the baby sees itself as the whole world. In the words of one psychologist, this is a case of "radical egocentrism—a complete lack of differentiation between himself and his actions and the characteristics of the given situation." The child will continue to be egocentric in later stages, but in the sensorimotor period, the sense of self and the surroundings are totally undifferentiated.

An infant's thought processes are dominated by events. This is Piaget's term for activities involving the senses and movement—looking, hearing, touching, sucking, and kicking. A vast amount of preliminary cognitive activity is also taking place, so much that Piaget felt obliged to divide the first 2 years of life into six stages. Each is characterized by progressively more elaborate arrangements of schemes.

Chapter 6

Stages of Reflexive Behavior

Stage one: reflexive behavior

The month after birth is dominated by the infant's reflexes: behavior and ability with which the child came already equipped from the womb. These are the child's first schemes. A prime example: the infant sucks when the lips are touched. This kind of activity is innate, unlearned.

Stage two: primary (first-level) circular reactions

At 2 to 3 months, the baby's actions, oriented to the body, are becoming repetitive; when an action is completed, it seems to stimulate its own recurrence. These primary circular reactions are thus characterized by purposeless, repetitive behavior. Sucking is different now. At the sight of a bottle, the infant sucks for the apparent pleasure of the activity, even if the nipple does not touch the mouth. No longer a reflex, sucking is now a primary circular reaction.

It is also a sign that a child has achieved object recognition. But according to Piaget, object permanence has not yet been achieved: if someone takes the bottle away, the baby forgets it. Likewise, a toy dropped from the crib is not only out of sight but out of mind. The infant looks at something else.

Piaget's analysis of what happens during this stage has been disputed by other psychologists, who contend that there is evidence that the infant may not really forget or that the forgetting may not be immediate. One experiment showed that infants still reached for objects that went out of sight when lights were turned out. And in another investigation, infants were repeatedly shown a cube, but each time its orientation in space was different. Eventually the babies became just as inattentive as if the cube had been offered over and over in exactly the same place. The researcher's conclusion was that the infants had demonstrated memory; otherwise, each sight of the cube should have elicited as much attention as when seen for the first time. The ability to become habituated to stimuli is an early sign of memory.

If mothers and fathers have taken an active role in caring for the child, they will have become "objects" to be recognized. And the baby may smile when they appear. Yet when Father or Mother leave the room, says Piaget, the baby will not seem to miss them.

Stage three: secondary (second-level) circular reactions

At 4 to 8 months, the focus of infants' interests moves from their own bodies to the environment. Children are becoming aware that what they do can have amusing consequences. Secondary circular reactions are characterized by activities that produce an interesting effect. The baby kicks, not for the sake of kicking, but to move the mobile overhead. Actions remain repetitive, or circular; the same thing will be done over and over again.

Another advance during this period is a baby's achievement of object permanence, one of the first milestones in cognitive development. As a result, a mother and father will begin to discover a gratifying new consequence of parenthood. The baby not only recognizes them when they appear, but is also starting to remember and miss them when they are out of sight. (This event is apt to take place in connection with the primary caregiver, usually the mother. As more and more fathers play a leading role in their babies' lives, they will also achieve early "father permanence.")

The baby's new accomplishment of missing the primary caregiver is really an occasion for rejoicing. The child is now able to make use of one more primary building block of thought: there is a scheme to represent an object—father or mother—that is not always present. It is this ability to retain a scheme for an unseen object that will later enable the child to deal with symbols, words, and mental representations.

Sixteen weeks is the earliest age for which investigators have experimentally confirmed object permanence. Eye movements were observed in a test of infants' ability to track a moving object. At one point, a screen hid the object from view. A baby who had attained object permanence would look at the other side of the screen for the object.

Piaget's work with older infants, also using a screen, revealed a developmental sequence. At 6 to 7 months, babies can find an object partially hidden from view. At 8 months, they can find a completely hidden object. However, if a child sees the object hidden at location A and then hidden again at location B, the infant looks for it at A. At 9 months, the child searches for the object at the point of its disappearance.

Stage four: coordination of secondary circular reactions

The period from 8 to 12 months is an extension of the previous stage. Earlier, actions were repeated because of their interesting effects. Now, we see an even more purposeful sort of activity—to achieve a desired result. Thus, coordination of secondary circular reactions involves goal-oriented activities. Because of a new ability to keep an object in mind—to formulate a scheme—the baby can now plan to achieve an end. This ability to seek goals is based on object permanence.

Parents now discover they must contend with an individual who has a mind of his own. Father is reading a letter with his son in his lap. Baby reaches for the letter. Father puts it in his shirt pocket: Baby reaches into the pocket and takes the letter out. The father puts the paper back into the pocket. The baby pulls it out as often as the father takes it away. This goal-oriented behavior illustrates one thing more: the child now has a rudimentary understanding of spatial relationships. The baby realizes that there is space in the pocket in which to put the letter.

During this period of a child's life, the concept of persons as permanent objects develop fast. Person permanence is probably one of the first signs of the development of object permanence. To a baby who is 8 to 11 months old, people are even more interesting than pieces of paper or other objects. The child focuses attention more on the caregiver than on inanimate objects. Person permanence in its earliest form is demonstrated by the infant who motions or moves toward the screen that is shielding a person from view.

Because of object or person permanence, the infant begins to recognize environmental discrepancies, such as strangers or the absence of a caregiver. The obvious clue is how they react to being left with a sitter. The worst reaction to being left with a sitter seems to come between 1 year and 15 months.

Jerome Kagan, who analyzed these differentiated age responses, believes that they reflect a baby's increasing ability, after 9 months, to formulate very simple hypothesis. The child can theorize about what happened to absent parents and whether or not they will come back. A year-old-baby can recognize a "different" event, is frightened, and has no idea why such a thing has happened. Later on, the child can figure out some answers and is less upset.

Kagan maintains that this sequence is the beginning of cognitive activity. He has some physiological evidence. He points out that an increase in heart rate in older children usually accompanies attentive, thoughtful behavior. Kagan, therefore, concludes that simple cognitive activities begin within Piaget's sensorimotor period (0–2 years), not afterward, as Piaget contends.

Stage five: tertiary (third-level) circular reactions

At 12 to 18 months, the toddler arrives at the trial-and-error stage. Tertiary circular reactions involve exploring all the potentialities of objects. The term tertiary is used to indicate that children's thoughts have progressed beyond their own bodies (primary circular reactions) to a third dimension. They are now using schemes acquired from previous stages to experiment with the varied possibilities of objects. All the experimentation is acted out. A square peg won't fit into a round hole. The child tries all the holes until one fits.

This is the period when the little one is "into everything"—pots scattered over the kitchen floor, little fingers reaching into the electric light sockets, toilet paper rolls unrolled. The baby is merely experimenting with all the wonderful objects in the domestic world, trying them out in all the ways that come to mind.

Piaget lays great stress on these sensorimotor activities. He maintains that they allow the child to interact with physical reality and to learn from and about the environment. A foundation is being laid for later conceptual development. The baby is learning concepts like "hard" and "soft," "cold" and "warm," "squashy," "round." All this is a veritable voyage of useful discovery.

Stage six: invention of new means through mental combinations

A child aged 18 to 24 months is sophisticated indeed. Through mental combinations, the child invents new ways to solve simple problems. It is no longer necessary to rely on trial and error to find the right hole for that square peg. The solution takes place in mind, rather than through the fingers. The child looks at the peg, surveys the holes, decides what matches by picturing it all in the mind, and then puts the peg into the right hole.

Mischief-making of the previous stage, while messy and noisy, is as nothing compared to this new era. Are there cookies on the shelf? The young thinker will look over the situation and figure out a plan: push a chair over to a strategic counter, climb on the chair, climb on the counter, and easily reach the can of cookies. This naughtiness is just the beginning of mental maturity and problem solving.

Preschool Years: Preoperational Thought

The age span from 2 to 7 years is termed preoperational by Piaget. The sensorimotor period has been left behind through maturation and equilibration. The preoperational child is still egocentric, and irreversibility continues. The child's world is concrete absolute. Orientation is global. The child is guided mostly by visual cues. Words are becoming important and beginning to stand for objects, but the objects are still more important. Interaction with the environment and with various people has provided the necessary stimulation to propel the preschooler into this new stage. However, children at this age have not matured sufficiently to deal with the world on any but absolute terms. Abstract concepts and relative terms still escape them.

Limitations still continue. Piaget's water level experiments reveal the limitations of younger children. They do not yet have the ability to conserve, to perceive that transformation in appearance does not alter quantity. Conservation reflects relativistic, reversible thinking. Children whose thought processes are basically egocentric do not conserve or reverse. Nor are children in this age range capable of classification, of mental division of a category into its component parts. They cannot think of parts and the whole at the same time.

A 4-year-old boy remarked, "I liked oranges when I lived in San Francisco, but not when I was in California." Intellectually, he was too young to grasp the fact that San Francisco and California belong to the same time frame.

Relative terms are almost meaningless to children of this age. They think in absolutes. They do not see people or things as darker, lighter, shorter, and taller. Objects are dark or light. People are tall or short. Ask a 4-year-old which of two tall uncles is taller. The decision is beyond the child.

Relationships are hard to deal with. A 4-year-old boy is asked: "Do you have a brother?" "Yes!" "What's his name?" "Jim." "Does Jim have a brother?" "No!"(Phillips 1969:61). That he can be his brother's brother is more than he can understand.

Most "bright sayings" date from this period when children are having difficulty understanding classification. "Do we eat turkey at Christmas?" "No, at dinner." "Is a dog an animal?" "No—he's a dog."

Everything is seen from the youngster's own point of view. The child is egocentric in perception as well as in thinking. This was illustrated by an experiment in which three different-sized "mountains" were placed on different parts of a table (Piaget and Inhelder 1956). The child sat in a chair facing one of the mountains. Given some cut-out drawings of what the occupants of each of the chairs might see from their vantage point and asked to choose which view would be seen from each chair, the child was baffled. It was difficult to imagine the situation from any other than the child's own point of view.

Preoperational children also demonstrate undifferentiated global behavior. The most overwhelming impression dominates their thinking, like the higher waterline in the glass-of-water game.

All these absolutes begin to break up between the ages of 4 and 7. During this transitional period, children begin to doubt their previously positive judgments. They start to consider other perspectives. With help from an adult, they can decenter their thinking. At times, they can grasp more than one aspect of a situation. The child is developing logic, and it is getting in the way of what was once clear, if mistaken, perceptions of how things are.

Some people question the validity of Piaget's theories because they wonder what part language plays in children's responses. When children give the wrong answers, isn't it possible that they are simply not understanding words like more or less? Some experimenters did find that some children used those two words when they were really referring to height and length. Another investigator found evidence that 4-year-olds equate big and tall, but only semantically. They know what big is but often use it to refer to height.

When asked, "Which is bigger?" preschoolers and first and second graders tend to rely heavily on the vertical dimension of objects. Their approach is unmistakably unidimensional. In judging quantity of liquids, the height of the container is the most salient cue for 6-year-olds. Thus, egocentrism decreases with age.

Another reason children frequently use height as a standard is that they are often exposed to height standards in daily life: pouring equal amounts of milk or soft drinks into glasses; using measuring cups; standing people back-to-back.

However, some studies have shown that language is not the handicapping factor for children who do not show conservation. Training in the words *more* or *less* does not necessarily improve conservation performance in 4-year-olds.

Investigators have duplicated Piaget's conservation of quantity experiments without using the two suspect terms. Instead of using jars of water, the experimenters showed children two equal-sized jars of candy. One jar had more candy than the other. Then the smaller amount of candy was poured into a taller, narrower jar so that the level was higher than that of the jar with more candy. The children were asked which jar of candy they would like, and why.

Conservers chose the jar that actually contained more, and supported their choice by commenting that there was more candy in it. The ages at which the children demonstrated conservation corresponded to Piaget's concrete operational stage 7 to 11.

A different study demonstrated that sixth-grade boys who used few hypothetical statements and had a poor command of language in general were no less able to think in hypothetical terms and to demonstrate formal operations ability than more verbal youngsters.

While these investigations seem to support Piaget's conclusion that language is not critical to cognitive development, the issue is still unresolved. Sixty-six English children around the age of 5 were given a three mountains test similar to Piaget's. The children were divided into four groups. Three groups were given three different kinds of training through movement, visual clues, and verbal clues to improve their performance. One control group got no extra training at all.

The experimenters found that a 5-year-old does not necessarily have to occupy another observer's position in order to describe the view from that place. The procedures used gave the children either visual or verbal information to aid them in the right answers.

Chapter 7

Preparing Educators to Work with Students from Diverse Backgrounds

The Redefinition of Teaching and Schooling Today

In three major studies, the Natural Science Foundation found that most science education follows the traditional practice: At all grade levels the old predominant method of teaching was recitation (discussion) with the teacher in control supplementing the lesson with new information (lecturing). The key to the information and basis for reading assignments was the textbook. If science is presented like this, is it any wonder that children's natural curiosity about their physical world turns into boredom by the time they leave grade school?

The Recitation Script

"Recitation": It is everywhere in North American schools. It is the most frequently reported form of interactive teaching (Hoetker and Ahlbrand 1969). "Recitation" has been described in the educational literature for over 90 years. It constitutes a major portion of all interactive teaching.

Recitation consists of a series of unrelated teacher questions that require convergent factual answers and student-known information. Recitation questioning seeks predictable, correct answers. It includes up to 20 percent of yes/no questions. Only rarely in recitation are teacher questions responsive to student productions. Only rarely are they used to assist students to develop more complete or elaborated ideas.

Other studies of interactive teaching are no more encouraging: Teachers are mainly guided by preselected activities and commonsense ideas about child development and educational practice. Teachers seldom report being reflective during interactions with students; they do not refer to educational theories, and they engage in little pedagogical maneuvering.

This dismal portrait describes not only the schools of time past, but some few unlucky or deprived communities of the present. Goodlad conducted a broadly based survey of 38 American schools in 13 communities and seven regions of the United States. Hundreds of students and teachers were interviewed and observed in small and large schools, in low- and middle-socioeconomic communities, in both rural and metropolitan areas with diverse cultural and ethnic populations.

Goodlad's researchers found a striking similarity in the seemingly diverse situations. For the most part, teachers controlled what transpired, and the focus was on the total group of students, rather than small groups or individuals. Teachers emphasized role learning and immediate responses. Most of the time, teachers lectured and explained; almost never were there opportunities for give-and-take between a challenging teacher and learning students. The student role was passive, and few teachers made any effort to adapt instructions to individual differences.

Sarason summarized previous studies of classrooms and reported that teachers frequently did quiz students in a favorite activity and frequently questioned them in large groups from 45 to 150 times per half hour. Unfortunately, they quizzed students in such a way that students responded with few questions of their own. The more questions asked by the teacher that are answerable by simple recall, the fewer questions children asked. When teachers asked personally relevant questions, children's questions increased. These rates were not different for students according to IQ or social class.

The recitation questioning pattern is supported by the educational apparatus at every level, including standard curriculum materials. A quote from Secretary Bennett's first lesson:

Classroom materials provided to teachers may frustrate their attempts ... Teacher manuals have embedded in the teachers' directions and questioning techniques ... Answers are right, wrong, but mostly short, thus, smothering the student's efforts to be an effective and intuitive thinker.

Recent Progress in the Reform of Teaching

In recent years, the "effective teacher" movement (based on process-product research) has succeeded in identifying existing classroom practices associated with greater student learning. On the whole, this movement is a salutary development, even though it suffers from being a theoretical one, which has constrained the movement to studies of existing practices, rather than experimenting with fresh forms.

Duffy and his associates summarized the works on teacher effectiveness and drew two conclusions: (a) the most effective teachers of basic skills generate the greatest opportunity to learn; (b) such teachers are technical managers of instructional materials and activities, rather than theory-driven and reflective decision makers.

They state that even in these "more effective" classrooms, there is little evidence of instruction of any kind. Teachers spend most of their time assigning activities, monitoring to be sure the pupils are on task, directing recitation sessions to assess how well children are doing, and providing corrective feedback in response to pupil errors. Seldom does one observe ... teaching in which a teacher presents a skill, a strategy, or a process to pupils, and shows them how to do it, provides assistance as they make initial attempts to perform the task, and assures that they can be successful.

Few writers would dispute the value of highly organized technical and direct forms of didactic instruction. Such classrooms are far more effective than those that rely on unstructured, informal teaching, where students have broad latitude to select what they will do. Among such practices associated with higher achievement are daily and weekly review, checking homework, correction of errors, and independent practice (seatwork).

"Time on task" or "engaged time" is another important factor: In the "technical" classroom, where "automatic teaching" is the norm, pupils are engaged on task for longer amounts of time and, thus, have more opportunity to learn. Not only is this intuitively sound, but educational research has repeatedly shown that time on task is a positive factor for student performance.

One can also make a case for a selective value of recitation and didactic instruction from cross-cultural literature. Memorization is widely and effectively used to teach sacred texts and rituals; other cultural knowledge may also be taught in this way.

For example, it is essential that students have "automatic" control of the alphabet and sound-symbol relationships, build "automatic" sight vocabulary, know essential facts of history (including dates), and internalize abstract categories.

For these abstract, symbolic, decontextualized forms of learning, various forms of didactic teaching may be the most effective, but they are not sufficient. They are particularly inadequate if students are to acquire some mastery and understanding of the knowledge and literature of the world's civilizations, that mastery that distinguishes the literate mind.

In its worst forms, "automatic" didactic teaching is little more than the recitation script of earlier eras. It emphasizes rote learning and students' passivity facts and low-level cognitive functions. It prevents implementation of many curricula. It can also contribute to poor morale because it diminishes the teacher role in order to make programs "teacher-proof." It works best with highly structured materials such as worksheets and "manufactured" reading materials.

Duffy remarked that however adaptive this "automatic" teaching may be in many classrooms contexts, it reflects inadequate training, the limits of current pedagogical theory, and an overreliance on commercial materials to the exclusion of real literature, art, and science. It also does little to promote intellectual development, cultural literacy, and thoughtful citizenship of the kinds that A Nation at Risk identified as crucial. We must develop ways of balancing "automatic" didactic teaching with teaching that assists learning. But does an alternative exist? Yes. Is "automatic" and didactic teaching the best we can do? No.

Teaching as Assistance
Another Kind of Teaching

The literature of U.S. educational research is filled with efforts to define and study interactive teaching that goes beyond recitation and "automatic" didactic teaching. Such teaching has been described in many ways, including guided practice and quality teaching.

In this literature, recurrent themes and positions can be discerned. Also in contemporary theory and research on behavior, cognition, and human development, there is theory ready at hand to explain and unify these many efforts to construct better teaching.

Our task is to review this theory and research and through it, to propose a reliable general teaching method. Through this theory and method, we then derive a general theory of schooling, a general theory of literacy, and consequently, a general theory of education.

Of what does this "other" kind of teaching consist? For one thing, it clearly involves subject-matter competence. To do more than merely manage activities and allow students to learn on their own, teachers must command the knowledge and skills they seek to impart. The point of teaching is to impart knowledge and the capacity to process that knowledge. In this respect, we come down fully on the context side of the debate over content versus process. Teachers and students, alike, must know the subject matter; they must learn the accumulated knowledge and important facts of our civilization and the world's cultures.

Pedagogical expertise is also required, of which there are many kinds, including instructional objectives, positive and efficient classrooms and behavior management, provision of effective and varied activities, properly conducted recitation and drills, orderly monitoring and assessment of progress, checking for comprehension, and any number of other expert practices. The fully professional teacher will command all of these useful and desirable practices and learn to apply them to those aspects of the curricula for which they are most efficient.

Numerous theories of teaching have been proposed in recent decades, many, of which, are embedded in broad "models" of educational performance that cover not only teaching but also learning, instruction, motivation, curriculum, and other processes. These efforts, combined with the steady accretion of understanding in the psychological, developmental, and social science, have made possible the unified theory of teaching and education that we propose.

The Basis for a Theory of Teaching and Schooling

Although social and behavioral research has never had much effect on the practice of teaching and schooling, its potential to guide change is now discernible. It is an emergent contextualist and interactionist view of human development that draws from the achievements of twentieth-century English-speaking social science. This had profound implications for teaching, schooling, and education.

A key feature of this emergent view of human development is that higher-order functions develop out of social interaction. vygotsky argued that a child's development cannot be understood by a study of the individual. We must also examine the external social world in which that individual life has developed.

Cognitive communicative skills appear twice, or in two plans. It appears on the social plan, and then on the psychological plan. It also appears between people as an intrapsychological category. Through participation in activities that require cognitive and communicative functions, children are drawn into the use of these functions in ways that nurture them.

Teaching is a life's journey, a series of goals, objectives related and unrelated, and diverse skills and activities. Teaching, then, must be redefined:

1. as assisting performance, and
2. as occurring when performance is achieved with assistance.

Planning Meaningful Curriculum
A Mini Story of Children and Teachers Learning Together

I firmly agree with the article about planning meaningful curriculums and what others had to say. They all believe that children are capable learners with many questions, ideas, feelings, and theories about their world. They also believe that teachers and young children are "co-learners" in the classroom who benefit from learning experiences that offer: 1) connections to their prior knowledge, 2) opportunities for observation, 3) opportunities to construct questions and hypothesis, and 4) time to revisit ideas and to reflect on their actions.

I find that all of these statements are true and must be included in all academic content standards and sprinkled throughout the curriculum.

In order for both teacher and student to benefit in a shared learning experience of this kind, there first must be a standard-based curriculum, such as The California Standards for the Teaching Profession, along with school district Academic Content Standards. Both standards are designed to empower students with academic skills, knowledge, confidence, and to become productive members of society.

The core curriculum must provide programs with a purpose, goals, and objectives to engage and support all students in learning, helping students to connect prior knowledge, life experiences, and interests with learning goals.

I also believe that in order to help all students reach their highest potential, teachers should establish and articulate goals for student learning with modifying instructional plans to adjust for student needs.

I appreciate the statement in the article that said observation plays a critical role in the development of a meaningful curriculum and that careful study of children's classroom behavior provides teachers with the information to plan connected learning experiences that build on children's interests and allow for continued inquiry. It further states that teachers may record their observations using photographs, videotapes, audiotapes, or written notes. Using this information collected, teachers can generate questions, formulate hypothesis, and propose the next steps for their curriculum.

I believe that understanding and organizing subject matter for student learning is very important, because some of these materials may be used as resources to make subject matter accessible to students.

Chapter 8

Methods of Psychological Research and Psychological Assessment

PSYCHOLOGISTS STUDY THE ABILITIES, NEEDS, and activities of human beings. Psychology is also related to the social sciences of anthropology and sociology, which deal with people in society. Like anthropologists and sociologists, psychologists investigate the attitudes and relationships of human beings in social settings. These three academic disciplines often study the same problems from different perspectives. Psychologists concentrate on individual behavior and are especially interested in the beliefs and feelings that influence a person's actions.

Psychologists use much the same approach as other scientists do. They develop theories, also called hypothesis, which are possible explanations for what they have observed. They, then, use scientific methods to test their hypothesis. The chief techniques used in psychological research include: (1) naturalistic observation, (2) systematic assessment, and (3) experimentation.

Naturalistic observation involves watching the behavior of human beings in their natural environment. It is a valuable source of information to psychologists. The research itself has less effect on the subjects' behavior than a controlled experiment does. But observation, alone, seldom proves a cause-and-effect relationship between two or more events. As a result, psychologists use naturalistic observation chiefly as an exploratory technique to gain insights and ideas for later testing.

Systematic Assessment is the general name for a variety of organized (systematic) methods used to examine (assess) people's thoughts, feelings, and personality traits. The chief types of systematic assessment include case histories, surveys, and standardized tests.

A *case history* is a collection of detailed information about an individual's past and present life.

A *survey* is a study that measures people's attitudes and activities by directly asking the people about their attitudes and activities. A psychologist conducting a survey prepares carefully worded questions. If the psychologist wishes to form general conclusions, the survey must collect responses from a representative sample of individuals.

A *standardized test* is an examination for which average levels of performance have been established and which has shown consistent results. In addition, uniform methods of administering and scoring the test have already been developed. Psychologists use such tests to help measure abilities, aptitudes, interests, and personality traits. For example, most students who plan to attend college take a standardized test called a college entrance examination during their junior or senior year in high school. This test measures some of the abilities thought to contribute to success in college.

Case histories, surveys, and standardized tests enable psychologists to gather much information that they could not detect by naturalistic observation.

Experimentation helps a psychologist discover, or confirm, cause-and-effect relationships in behavior. In a typical experiment, the researcher divides subjects at random into two groups, one called the experimental group and the other the control group. For the experimental group, the researcher changes one condition that is likely to affect the subjects' behavior and holds all other factors constant. The experimenter does nothing to control the group. If the experimental group behaves differently from the control group, the one condition changed probably caused the difference in behavior.

The experimental method enables scientists to test a theory under controlled conditions. But many psychologists hesitate to form conclusions based only on laboratory investigation. In many cases, people's behavior changes simply because they know they are part of an experiment.

Modern psychology has incorporated many teachings of the earlier schools. For example, though many psychologists disagree with certain of Freud's ideas, most accept his concept that the unconscious plays a major role in shaping behavior. Similarly, most psychologists agree with the behaviorists that the environment influences behavior and that they should study chiefly observable actions. However, many psychologists object to pure behaviorism because it pays too little attention to such processes as reasoning and personality development.

Psychology Today

A group of extreme behaviorists called the stimulus-response school believe all behavior is a series of responses to different stimuli. According to these psychologists, the stimulus connected with any response can eventually be identified. As a result, stimulus-response psychologists regard behavior as predictable and potentially controllable.

Another group of psychologists, who are known as the cognitive school, believe there is more to human nature than a series of stimulus-response connections. These psychologists concentrate on such mental processes as thinking, reasoning, and self-awareness. They investigate how a person gathers information about the world, processes the information, and plans responses.

A school called humanistic psychology developed as an alternative to behaviorism and psychoanalysis. Humanistic psychologists believe individuals are controlled by their own values and choices and not entirely by the environment, as behaviorists think, or by unconscious drives, as psychoanalysis believes. The goal of humanistic psychology is to help people function effectively and fulfill their own unique potential. Those supporting this approach include the American psychologists, Abraham H. Maslow and Carl R. Rogers. Many psychologists do not associate themselves with a particular school or theory; instead, they select and use what seems best from a variety of sources. This approach is called eclecticism.

A child's psychological growth depends on his or her environment. Environment consists of everything with which a child comes in regular or frequent contact, including other people. The majority of children receive the environmental help they need for normal psychological development.

However, psychological growth is also affected by physical factors. For example, advances in learning ability are influenced by the development of the nervous system. Children do not develop physically at the same rate. As a result, their readiness for psychological growth also varies. Thus, a child who develops at a somewhat slower rate than average is not necessarily abnormal.

Childhood can be divided into four stages based on periods of major psychological change. These stages are: (1) the toddler stage, (2) the preschool years, (3) the early school years, and (4) the preteen years.

The toddler stage lasts from about 18 months to 3 years of age. A child's physical growth is generally slower during this second 18 months after birth than it was during the first 18 months.

By 18 months of age, most children can feed themselves, walk, and run a short distance, stack some blocks, and say a few meaningful words. A toddler is expected to improve all these skills. But the development of language skills, especially the building of sentences, is a major challenge. Most 2 year olds use one or two words for an entire thought. By 3 years of age, however, most children can link several words together to form a fairly complete sentence. They can speak about 900 words—an enormous increase over the average 10- to 20-word vocabularies at 18 months of age.

Toddlers also vastly improve their powers of imitation and imagination. Some kinds of imitation are fun and attract attention, such as imitating the sounds that animals make. Most toddlers have an active imagination and love to pretend. They may pretend that a cup of water is a cup of tea or that a tricycle is an automobile.

A toddler's social relationships develop slowly. Until children are about 2 years old, they tend to be shy around other youngsters. Children usually overcome their shyness after a few minutes, though they may still consider another child more as an object than as a person. By 3 years of age, children start to realize that they have things in common with other children. They then begin to regard them as equals.

Toddlers form their strongest attachments to their parents or substitute parents. In most cases, the mother is especially looked to for help, comfort, and companionship. The majority of children in Western societies have fewer contacts with the father, though they respect and imitate him. Above all, toddlers want to feel assured that they have their parents' acceptance and approval. As a result, they are sensitive to any sign of rejection or disapproval.

The preschool years extend from about 3 to 5 years of age. This period helps prepare children for the degree of independence and responsibility they will be given during the next stage of childhood, the early school years. Preschoolers are highly active and constantly exploring the world around them. At the same time, they are beginning to learn that there are certain standards of behavior they should and should not do.

By about 3 or 4 years of age, the majority of children have become increasingly aware of themselves and of other people. They are not only more conscious of their own actions, but they have also begun to realize that other people have feelings like their own. Children then start to govern some of their actions according to the pleasure or displeasure that they give another person.

Most parents use rewards and punishments to teach their children standards, or behavior. They reward children for desired actions and punish them for undesired ones. A word of praise or a hug is usually a sufficient reward. Punishment usually consists of a strong "no," and gradually, a child learns that some behaviors are bad. In most cases, however, it is the parents who must decide the goodness or badness of an action.

Preschoolers also learn standards of behavior through a more or less unconscious process called identification. The process often begins during the toddler stage, but it becomes fully developed during the preschool years. Children identify with another person if they feel that they have the same physical and psychological characteristics as that person. Most children identify with one or more members of their family, especially their parents.

The majority of 3 and 4 year olds do not know they have a choice in their actions. If something they do displeases their parents, they feel anxious, ashamed, or sorry. But they do not blame themselves for the action. By about 5 years of age, however, most children start to realize that they can choose one action rather than another. Children then begin to feel guilt, as well as shame, if they behave wrongly.

The early school years, which last from about age 5 to 8, mark a major turning point in a child's psychological development. Children continue to improve their physical skills during this stage. But the period is distinguished mainly by important advances in a child's mental, emotional, and social development.

In most societies, children have been taught basic standards of social behavior by their fifth year. They are also learning to judge whether particular actions are right or wrong. A child can thus be given more independence. However, adults channel this independence along definite lines. In the United States and most other developed countries, children must start school at about 5 or 6 years of age.

Every schoolchild is expected to learn to solve problems, a skill that improves with practice. A 5 year old may try to solve a problem by choosing the first solution that comes to mind. But a 6 or 7 year old thinks about other possible solutions and recognizes why one is better than another. Children of this age also begin to see how they differ.

Finally, children gain confidence in their mental powers and start to enjoy solving problems correctly.

By the age of 7 or 8, most children begin to rationalize their beliefs—that is, to find reasons for holding them. They may thus decide that the standards of behavior they have learned are good standards to hold. Children this age also increasingly compare themselves with other youngsters. Such comparisons contribute to a child's self-image. The self-image that they develop during childhood can influence their behavior throughout life.

Children begin to form a self-image during the preschool years as they identify with their parents or other family members. A child's self-image is favorable or unfavorable, depending on the attitudes and emotions of the persons with whom the child identifies. For example, children who see mainly negative qualities in their parents will likely view themselves in a negative light. Children form a more favorable self- image if they have a better impression of their parents. When children compare themselves with other children, they reinforce or alter their basic self-image.

Heredity and Environment

Two, main forces—heredity and environment—account for the individual differences among children. Heredity is the process by which children inherit physical and mental traits from their parents. Environment consists of all the things in a child's surroundings that affect the child's development of the inherited traits.

Individual differences among children are caused by heredity and environment acting together, not separately. In general, heredity limits what the environment can do in influencing a child's development. For example, every child inherits a tendency to grow a certain height. Not even the best environmental conditions will enable a child to grow much taller than this height. But children need the right conditions, including proper nourishment and exercise, to grow as tall as their heredity allows. Heredity and environment together, thus, determine the physical differences among children. The two forces together also account for individual differences in intelligence.

Differences in intelligence among children are usually measured by IQ (intelligence quotient) tests. These tests are designed to indicate a child's general mental ability in relation to other children of the same age. Each child's performance on the tests is rated by an IQ score. About two-thirds of all children score from 84 to 116. About a sixth score below 84, and a sixth score above 116.

The IQ scores of persons related by blood generally differ less than do the scores of unrelated persons. Some experts therefore conclude that general mental ability is only slightly affected by environment. Other experts, however, believe that environment has a strong influence on a person's intelligence. Their view is supported by studies of culturally deprived children. Children are considered culturally deprived if their home life lacks the kinds of experiences that will help them profit from formal schooling. Many such children have an IQ score below 80. But in a number of cases, culturally deprived children have dramatically improved their score after receiving special training and encouragement in school.

Some experts question the usefulness of IQ tests on the grounds that they do not measure basic mental skills. These experts point out that intelligence involves a variety of separate powers, such as memory, logic, evaluation, and originality. A child may have little ability in some of these areas, but exceptional talent in one or more of the other areas. The critics, therefore, believe that children should be tested and evaluated for each mental skill separately.

Chapter 9

Lesson Plan Samples

Regions 8 & 11 Professional Development Consortia

Test #: *Velma Melancon*

Cover Sheet for a Lesson Plan

Each teacher must submit two different lesson plans

Teacher : Velma Melancon	*Grade:* Kindergarten
Content Area: Mathematics	
Objective(s): Students will use Gummy Bears to count, sort, and tally to construct a graph.	
Materials: Assorted Gummy Bears and individual worksheets	

Language Proficiency Levels: LEP I

Rubric 3 was used in Content, Teaching & Learning Strategies. Students' Experiences and Observations of students and their Language usage. SDAIE lesson and cooperative grouping for this activity.

List your desired outcomes for this multiple-day lesson (language and content).

Students were actively involved in many hands-on activities and experiences. They were able to create a graph from data and made guesses/predictions. Identify and sort by colors, classify by color and tally.

- Explain how this lesson provides evidence of meeting the outcomes you listed above.

    Students were able to count numbers 1–50. Students were able to write numbers 1–50.

    Students were able to identify colors and read color words. They were able to classify, color pictures, and tally numbers to show how many colors there were.

- What else would you like the readers to know about this lesson and your use of SDAIE strategies?

    Cooperative grouping is the key to sharing knowledge and exploring activities that cannot be completed in one day. It is also excellent for comparing groups.

LESSSON PLAN SAMPLES

Teacher: *Velma Melancon*
Student Work Sample Cover Sheet

The student work consists of THREE different examples of ONE student's work that shows the development of a sample concept, theme, or unit.
Complete the cover sheet and attach the samples of student work.

Content Area: MATH	English Language Level (circle one) Beginning Intermediate Advanced
Grade Level: *Kindergarten*	Primary Language: *LEP I*

- Briefly explain the content of the unit, theme, or concept each sample was taken from.
  This lesson was developed from "Primarily Bears, Book I, by AIMS Education Foundation.

- What is the objective and purpose for each sample of student work included?
  Sample 1   *Students to observe color and color words for counting and recording Gummy Bears on graph.*
  Sample 2   *Students sort out Gummy Bears and line them up building a graph by forming colors.*
  Sample 3   *Build a real graph by coloring the space of the different colors according to the candy in their cups.*

- What examples of teaching learning strategies were used during the assignment?
  Estimation by having students guess the number of bears that are in the jar. Listening, speaking, reading, and writing.

- How was the student's prior knowledge used?
  Students looked around the classroom for colors of the M&Ms. Counted how many different colors they named. They determined which had the highest number and which had the least number.

- What would you change or modify? (Suggest any revisions that would make this assignment better.)
  The lesson plan went well with cooperative learning/whole groups. Extended activities are the key for further learning and experience.

- What would you like readers to know about these samples which reflect SDAIE teaching?
  SDAIE STRATEGIES were very helpful in getting students engaged in critical thinking skills from the beginning to the end of the lesson.

Regions 8 & 11 Professional Development Consortia

Teacher: Velma Melancon

SDAIE
Teacher Lesson Plan

The two lesson plans submitted should be for multiple days and include the following: an introductory activity, objectives, and a description of the teacher/student interactions, an assessment component and grouping strategies. The lesson plans should demonstrate the ability to use SDAIE strategies in the classroom.

Introductory Activity

Students were shown a jar with M&M candies to guess the number of candies in the jar.

Objectives

To teach children how to count colors and graph them.

Context Clues (Materials Used, Teacher Behaviors, etc.)

1. Students were given a Gummy Bear sorting sheet to color
2. A counting sheet to color Bears
3. A tally sheet to tell how many in all
4. A counting chart
5. Gummy Bears in small Ziploc bags
6. Crayons
7. Pencils
8. Paper
9. Clear tape

Vocabulary, Listening, Speaking, Reading and/or Writing Activities

Counting, graphing, sorting, tally, guessing.
- Listening: Count Gummy Bears in baggies
- Speaking: Discuss data with a friend
- Reading: Word Bank
- Writing: Write a sentence to tell about the lesson or draw pictures

Teaching/Learning Strategies—Real-Life Applications

Check for understanding. Level of voice. Monitor and modeling. Real-life applications, students make a graph of colors each person wore and record the highest number.

Grouping Strategies

- Cooperative Grouping. Whole Group and Pair Share

Assessment

- Personal journals, attitude, observation, Rubric for Lesson Plan #3

PRIOR KNOWLEDGE

Teacher introduced color words from the word wall to the whole class. Students were able to read color words. A counting chart was used for students to count orally from 1–50. We talked about colors. Students looked around the classroom for colors of the M&Ms, such as blue, red, orange, green, brown, etc. We discussed how many of the colors they found in the classroom and also looked at each other's clothes to see who was wearing colors that were discussed. Students made guesses as to what colors had the highest and lowest count. Colors were counted, and the guessing game was over.

I. INTRODUCTORY ACTIVITY

Today, we are going to play a guessing game. We are going to look at the jar and guess how many Gummy Bears are in the jar. The number is more than eight and less than 30. The teacher shows students the jar with the Gummy Bears inside, then gives each student a small piece of paper to write the number on and their name. After all students have finished and the teacher checks for understanding, the students take their number and put it on the chart. The student whose number guess was closest to the actual number was the winner.

II. OBJECTIVES

Students will use Gummy Bears to construct a graph by:
1. Sorting Bears by color
2. Counting and charting Bears by color
3. Tallying Bears by color

III. CONTEXT CLUES

MATERIALS USED:
- Assortment of Gummy Bears randomly portioned into small Ziploc bags.
- Approximately 1–30 per bag.
  - Wall Chart
  - Crayons
  - Gummy Bears (candy)
  - Ziploc bags
  - Pencils
  - Clear tape to attach the number and name to the guessing chart and jar

- Gummy Bears sorting chart
- Gummy Bears tally and recording sheet
- Gummy Bears counting and color graph
- Writing journals

IV. TEACHER BEHAVIOR:

- Teacher checks for understanding
- Elicit student responses
- Signals "thumbs-up," "thumbs-down"
- Models and gives examples
- Monitors

V. VOCABULARY

- Counting
- Graphing
- Classifying
- Recording data
- Estimating
- Tally

VI. LISTENING

Students will listen and follow directions:
1. Count the Gummy Bears in your baggie
2. Sort out Gummy Bears according to color and place on graph paper
3. Build a real graph of bears by color
4. Place one Bear in each square
5. Look at each bear and color
6. Think about the colors. Which Bear has the most colors? Which Bear has the least?

VII. SPEAKING

- Discuss your data with a friend, sharing and comparing with each other.

VIII. READING

Look at the word bank and find the color words you used in your graph describing the number of Bears you had in each color. Read with your friend and share. For each color, what is the greatest and the least number?

IX. WRITING

Write a short sentence describing your graph using color and number words in your sentence. (Students may draw pictures to illustrate.) Record in the writing journals. The teacher must check for understanding.

X. TEACHING/LEARNING STRATEGIES

- Listening
- Speaking
- Reading
- Writing
- Cooperative Grouping
- Realia
- Prior Knowledge
- Vocabulary
- Word Bank
- Graphing Worksheet
- Color Sheet
- Questions/Answer Sheet

XI. REAL-LIFE APPLICATIONS

Students will create a graph of colors of the clothing each child is wearing in class. Use the same graph to look for colors that are the same. Divide the class into cooperative learning groups of four. Discuss the findings and share with another group. Teacher monitors this activity and checks for understanding. The teacher listens to each group's report. Finally, each group reports to the whole class.

XII. QUESTIONS

Students will graph the results of the Gummy Bears and chart on graphing paper and answer the following questions.

1. How many Gummy Bears did you find in your cup?
2. What color did you find more of than any others?
3. If you bought another bag of candy, would you find the same number of each color of candy? Why? Why not?

Teacher distributes the candy for all students to eat and enjoy.

XIII. GROUPING STRATEGIES

- COOPERATIVE GROUPING
- WHOLE GROUP
- PAIR SHARE

XIV. ASSESSMENT

- Personal Journals
- Portfolios
- Writing Sample
- Checking for Understanding
- Performance Tasks
- Attitude

- Observation
- Rubric for Lesson Plan #3

WORD BANK	
Counting	Green
Guess	Orange
Compare	Red
Graphing	Light Brown
	Dark Brown

LISTENING

Listen to the teacher give directions and explain procedures to follow.

SPEAKING

Discuss/Compare data on the bar graph with a friend.

READING

Read words from the word bank.

WRITING

Write or draw pictures in the personal math journals.

Regions 8 & 11 Professional Development Consortia
Name: *Velma Melancon*

Cover Sheet for a Lesson Plan
Each teacher must submit two different lesson plans

Teacher:	*Velma Melancon* Grade: *Kindergarten*
Content Area:	*Language Arts—Sequencing*
Objective(s):	*Identify sequence of events in story/sequence pictures to retell story.*
Materials:	*Storyboard. Incomplete sentences. Story Chart*

Language Proficiency Levels: Level 3

Students' work demonstrates adequate evidence of challenging content which is appropriate to grade level and the state framework. The reading/writing required is mostly appropriate to each student's language stage.

List your desired outcomes for this multiple-day lesson (language and content).

This lesson shows that there is an adequate degree of congruence between the student work and the objective of the lesson. The outcome shows the exposure of many activities (extended) that goes to, through, and beyond the text.

- Explain how this lesson provides evidence of meeting the outcomes you listed above.

  This lesson provided many learning experiences that included Total Physical Response extended activities, cooperative grouping, and real-life experiences with related activities. The students' work is mostly relevant and meaningful to their own experiences.

- What else would you like the readers to know about this lesson and your use of SDAIE strategies?

  It takes a lot of time to plan and develop a lesson of this nature. However, I am accustomed to planning highly sequential developed lessons. In order for students to perform at their very highest level of achievement, a lesson (SDAIE) with extended activities is appropriate.

Teacher: Velma Melancon

Student Work Sample Cover Sheet

The student work consists of **THREE** different examples of ONE student's work that shows the development of a sample concept, theme, or unit.

Complete the cover sheet and attach the samples of student work.

Content Area: LANGUAGE ARTS	English Language Level (circle one) Beginning Intermediate Advanced
Grade Level: *Kindergarten*	Primary Language: *Spanish*

- Briefly explain the content of the unit, theme, or concept each sample was taken from.

  L.U.S.D. Portfolio Assessment Guide, English Language Arts with suggested Core literature Caps for Sale, including the writing process. Summary of prompt scoring guide and domains of language. Listening, speaking, reading, and writing.

- What is the **objective** and **purpose** for each sample of student work included?

  Sample 1   *Identify sequence of events in a story.*
  Purpose: *To help students to understand order.*
  Sample 2   *To retell a story, using a creative storyboard.*
  Purpose: *To help student to understand that stories have a beginning, a middle, and an end.*
  Sample 3   *Story structure, plot sequence, completes the sentences to tell what happened first, next, and last.*

Purpose: *To show the sequence of the story.*

- What examples of teaching and learning strategies were used during the assignment?

  Cooperative four-person groups, vocabulary worksheet (individual), animal wall chart, created pictures, sentence strips, realia, story words, Venn diagram, and other extended activities.

- How was the student's prior knowledge used?

  Students were asked if they had ever visited a zoo or had seen animals in pictures or movies, and if they had ever seen people selling something on the streets.

- What would you **change** or **modify**? (Suggest any revisions that would make this better.)

  I would suggest only one objective and purpose for the lesson. I recommend that lessons be well developed with additional activities for growth.

- What would you like readers to know about these samples which reflect SDAIE teaching strategies?

  These samples include the four domains of Language, Listening, Speaking, Reading, and Writing. They also include SDAIE strategies and LUSD content standards and HBJ Language Arts program that support some of the strategies used in SDAIE. Both provide unit content, unit planning, unit resources, and themes.

SDAIE LESSON PLAN

Rubric 3

THEME: CAPS FOR SALE

A tale of a peddler, some monkeys, and their monkey business.
TOLD AND ILLUSTRATED BY: Esphyr Slobodkina
A Core Literature book selected for kindergarten students by
L.U.S.D.
SUBJECT: Language Arts
GRADE LEVEL: Kindergarten
LANGUAGE CLASSIFICATION: L.E.P. I.
PRESENTED BY: VELMA MELANCON
Abbott Elementary School

Regions 8 & 11 Professional Development Consortia

Teacher: *Velma Melancon*

SDAIE

Teacher Lesson Plan

The two lesson plans submitted should be for multiple days and include the following: an introductory activity, objectives, a description of the teacher/student interactions, an assessment component, and grouping strategies. The lesson plans should demonstrate the ability to use SDAIE strategies in the classroom.

Introductory Activity

The teacher asks students questions for discussion, like "Have you ever seen people selling things on the street?" Students talk about what they saw and heard. Teacher introduces the Big Book Caps for Sale by Esphyr Slobodkina. The teacher shows students the front cover and students are to discuss pictures.

Objectives

1. Students will identify the sequence of events in a story.
2. Students will use a storyboard to sequence pictures that retell the story showing the beginning, middle, and end.

Context Clues (Materials Used, Teacher Behaviors, etc.)

Wall chart	Teacher behavior
Storyboard	Modeling
Sentence strips	Check for understanding
Picture cards	Quality of voice

Vocabulary, Listening, Speaking, Reading and/or Writing Activities

Vocabulary used was story words, color, cut out, match, and paste. Words to match with picture are: peddler, monkeys, caps, and tree. (Each child has his or her individual worksheet.)

Teaching/Learning Strategies—Real-Life Applications

Students practiced wearing more than one hat. Cooperative grouping. Creative story writing/drawing. Story map, sequencing, sentence strips, vocabulary, Venn diagram, Domains of Language: listening, speaking, reading, and writing.

Grouping Strategies

Cooperative grouping where children were seated in groups of four and given a large piece of paper to divide into four boxes for each student, who then draws a picture about how the peddler looked when he sat under the tree to rest.

Assessment

Performance Task Portfolios. Teacher observation, writing samples, personal journals, conversations, Rubrics for lesson plan.

DAY 1

I. PRIOR KNOWLEDGE

Discuss/Questions: Teachers ask the following questions to the students:
1. How many of you have ever visited the zoo?
2. How many of you have seen animals in pictures?
3. How many of you have seen animals in movies?
4. Teacher makes a chart entitled:

ANIMALS WE HAVE SEEN
ELEPHANT
LION
TIGER
ZEBRA
MONKEY

5. Teacher records student's response on the animal chart and lists the names of animals they have seen at the zoo, in movies, or in pictures. The teacher invites students to tell what they know about the animal. The teacher asks students to name their favorite animal or pet. After students respond, the teacher asks them, "If you could be any animal you wanted to be, which animal would you choose?"
6. The teacher then asks students to explain how they are like the animal they choose.
7. Teacher checks for understanding. Teacher models for students by saying, "If I could be any animal I wanted to be, I would be a giraffe, because I am tall."

8. After teacher models the answer, students are encouraged to role play or act out their favorite animal.

BACKGROUND INFORMATION

SDAIE

This lesson is designed for L.E.P. students who are not fluent in English. It concentrates on activities that teach content areas, vocabulary skills, provides activities to develop higher level thinking skills, provides comprehensible input, role playing, games, charts, and description and sequencing of events. Use a variety of pictures and realia. Engage students in the domains of: language: listening, speaking, reading, and writing.

DAY 2

II. INTRODUCTORY ACTIVITY

Teacher asks students the following question for discussion:

1. Have you ever seen people selling things on the streets?
2. Students talk about what they saw and heard.

The teacher introduces the Big Book entitled *Caps for Sale*. The teacher shows children the front cover, reads the title, and tracks the print. Teacher points to the names of the author and illustrator. Then the teacher checks for understanding. The teacher reads the subtitle, *A Tale of a Peddler, Some Monkeys and Their Monkey Business*. Teacher asks the children if they know what a peddler is and what *monkey business* means. If they don't know, tell them to listen to the story.

DAY 3

SYNOPSIS

Caps for Sale by Esphyr Slobodkina is an amusing tale of a peddler who sells caps by stacking the caps on top of his head, walking down the street, and calling out, "Caps for sale!" One day, he awakens from a nap to discover his caps are gone. He looks up to find a tree full of monkeys with each monkey wearing a cap. He angrily pleads with the monkeys to return his caps, but they just imitate him. The frustrated peddler finally throws down his cap and begins to walk away, prompting the copycat monkeys to throw down their caps. The peddler gathers his caps, arranges them neatly on his head, and continues his familiar call—"Caps! Caps for sale! Fifty cents a cap!"

The teacher reads the story the first time aloud and asks the children to just listen. Then, the teacher rereads the story and chooses from the following activities for the children to do.

- Have children listen for the words the peddler repeats.
- Ask the children if they think this story could really have happened. Have them explain why or why not.
- Tell the children to think about the monkeys and what they do.

The teacher will write on chart paper the following words that may or may not describe the monkeys:

good	mean	curious
bad	funny	sad
playful	angry	happy

The teacher reads the words and asks the children to explain why they think each word does or does not describe the monkeys.

- The teacher asks the children if they think the peddler likes his job. Have them explain their reasoning.
- Discuss when and where the story takes place.

The teacher asks the following questions:

- Do you think the story took place a long time ago? Or this year?
- What clues from the story helped you decide?
- Is it in a "big" city or a "small" town?
- What clues from the story helped you decide?

DAY 4

III. OBJECTIVES

1. Students will identify the sequence of events in a story.
2. Students will draw and sequence pictures to retell the story in three parts: the beginning, middle, and end.
3. Students will complete sentences to tell what happened first, next, and last.

IV. CONTEXT CLUES

MATERIAL USED:

- Wall Chart

- Storyboard
- Big Book
- Animal Pictures
- Venn Diagram
- Sentence Strips
- Story Map
- Sequencing

TEACHER BEHAVIOR: Articulate clearly, speak slowly, utilize visual aids, modeling, and checking for understanding.

DAY 5

V. VOCABULARY

Caps for Sale

Story Words: Peddler, monkeys, caps, and trees

Directions: Children color pictures, cut out pictures, and match and paste pictures *(Individual Worksheet)*. The teacher checks for understanding and monitors activities.

DAY 6

VI. LISTENING

The teacher introduces a game called **Cap Cards** to the students. The teacher makes a set of cards in the shape of a cap. Each set should have 12 cards, three each of red, gray, blue, and brown.

The teacher groups the class into cooperative learning teams of four students and assigns the following tasks for the groups to complete.

Group I

The teacher tells the students to arrange the caps in the same order that the peddler wore them on his head. Each student should be responsible for one color. The teacher checks and monitors.

Group II

The teacher gives directions to this group and tells Group II to arrange the caps in the following pattern: 1 brown, 1 blue, 1 red, and 1 gray. Each student is responsible for one color. Students respond.

Group III

The teacher gives directions to Group III to arrange the caps in the following pattern: 2 reds, 2 grays, 2 blues, and 2 browns. Each student is responsible for one color. The teacher checks for understanding and monitors.

Group IV

The teacher gives directions. The teacher tells the students in Group IV to arrange the caps in a pattern of their own. Team members should cooperate in deciding on the pattern. Group discussions for the assignment.

Caps for Sale

Cooperative Learning/Listening/Speaking Problems

MONKEY AND CAP GAMES	
	Cap Pattern
Cap Cards: Make sets of cards in the shape of a cap. Each set should have 12 cards: three each of red, grey, blue, and brown. You may wish to use the pattern on this card. Group the class into cooperative learning teams of four students each. Assign the following tasks for the groups to complete.	
1. Arrange the caps in the same order that the peddler wore on his head. Each student should be responsible for one color.	
2. Arrange the caps in this pattern: 1 brown, 1 blue, 1 red, 1 gray. Each student is responsible for one color.	
3. Arrange the caps in this pattern: 2 red, 2 grays, 2 blues, 2 browns. Each student is responsible for one color.	
4. Arrange the caps in a pattern of your own. Team members should cooperate in deciding on the pattern. Ask other teams to identify your pattern.	

Listening and Speaking: Play a version of Simon Says to challenge students' listening and reacting skills. Explain the game Monkey Says as follows: one person is the monkey who gives orders that all the other monkeys must obey. The monkey leader acts out each order as it is given. However, the orders must be worded: "*Monkey says* point your finger." If the words "Monkey says" are omitted, then the others should not follow the order even if the leader performs the action.	

DAY 7

VII. LISTENING AND SPEAKING

The teacher engages students in a version of Simon Says to challenge students' listening and reacting skills. The teacher explains the game to the students. The teacher checks for understanding. Instead of saying, "Simon Says," say, "Monkey says."

One person volunteers to be the monkey who gives the orders that all monkeys must obey. The monkey leader acts out each order as it is given. However, the orders must be worded: "Monkey Says" point your finger. If the words "Monkey Says" are omitted, then the others should not follow the order, even if the leader performs the action.

DAY 8

VIII. READING ACTIVITIES

SENTENCE STRIPS:

The teacher uses a pocket chart and sentence strips for this reading activity that uses the peddler's words.

The teacher introduces sentences to the students. The teacher reads the first two sentences aloud and tracks the print and points to the picture words. Then the teacher asks the students to read them with her as she points to the pictures and the words. The teacher repeats the activity several times, encouraging the children to sound like a peddler. The teacher follows the same procedures for the last two sentences. Point out to the students that the peddler's words changed slightly as he grew angrier. The teacher asks the students to act out this part of the story to show how the peddler looked when he was angry. The teacher rereads the sentences again. This time, the teacher asks the students to add the words **better** or **must** before the word give. The teacher asks the students to try to sound angrier each time. Teacher pauses and checks for understanding.

IX. WRITING ACTIVITIES

The teacher asks the students what they would want to sell if they were peddlers. Children discuss what they would sell if they were peddlers. The teacher gives each student a piece of story paper. Have the children draw themselves selling the item they have chosen to sell. The teacher writes this on the board, reads to the students, then has the students read the words together. Students draw pictures where the lines are blank.

_____!
_____! For sale!

DAY 9

X. TEACHING/LEARNING STRATEGIES

- T.P.R.
- Sequencing
- Signals: Thumbs-up/Thumbs-down
- Venn Diagram
- Portfolio
- Realia
- Individual Worksheet
- Animal Wall Chart
- Model and Give Examples
- Video "Caps for Sale"
- Monitoring
- Storyboard
- Elicit Student Responses
- Story Word Activity Sheet
- BIG BOOK Caps for Sale
- Prior Knowledge
- Check for Understanding
- Sentence Strips
- Incomplete Sentences
- Cooperative/Heterogeneous Grouping
- Vocabulary

- Journals
- Visual Aids
- Word Bank
- K.W.L.

Domains of Language

1. Listening
2. Speaking
3. Reading
4. Writing

The teacher asks the students if they have a favorite cap or if they have a cap like the peddler. Students respond by sharing and describing their cap with a friend. The teacher asks the students if they would like to create a different cap or hat than the one they described and shared with a friend.

The teacher checks for understanding and monitors activities, walking around the room while checking for understanding. If students are unable to write, the teacher will write the sentence for the student, filling in the items being sold or spell the words for the student and have him/her copy the frame to complete the sentence.

LISTENING

Students play a game of Simon Says to challenge their listening and reacting skills. Change the name to "Monkey Says."

SPEAKING

Students use angry voices to act out words the peddler said.

READING
Students will read from sentence strips. Use the peddler's words.

WRITING
Students write or dictate what they would sell if they were peddlers. Draw pictures of them to illustrate.

REAL-LIFE APPLICATIONS

Students responded by using the signal "thumbs-up" or "thumbs-down." They all agreed to make a special cap/hat.

Students will need the teacher's help in making this special cap/hat. Materials needed for this activity per child are as follows:

>Realia
>1" x 22" strips of tagboard
>scrap paper

Materials for decorating: crayons, markers, paint, yarn, paper clips, stapler, and tape.

Teacher directions: Give children two paper plates and have them decorate the bottom of each plate. Teacher monitors and checks for understanding. The teacher tells children that one of the plates will be the bottom of their cap and should be colored only along the ridged border. The teacher models by placing two plates together with the decorations on the outside and staple along the edge, two-thirds of the way around the plates. The teacher helps the children to lightly stuff the plates with wadded-up scrap paper. Teacher then staples shut the remaining portion. Teacher uses cardboard strips to make the band and fasten it with a paper clip after placing the tagboard on the child's head. The teacher adjusts the band to fit the child's head. Then remove the paper clip and staple the band in place. The teacher tapes the band to the bottom plate in three places to help the child complete the cap.

The teacher raises this question for students to think about and respond to:

QUESTION:

Do you think it would be hard for the peddler or for themselves to balance so many caps on the top of their head?

The teacher gives students two opportunities to try.

Students try to balance each other's hats on their head and walk around the room without dropping a hat. The teacher continues to add more hats to discover how many hats the children can balance on their heads. The winner receives a free choice of activity time using the learning centers.

XI. GROUPING STRATEGIES

Cooperative/Heterogeneous Grouping

The teacher arranges children in sitting groups of four. Students respond. The teacher helps each group to divide the paper into four boxes by folding paper. The teacher checks for understanding. Teacher models and monitors behavior showing examples when needed.

Teacher directions: In box 1, teacher discusses with students what they are about to do. Checks for understanding. Use signals "thumbs-up" or "thumbs-down" for correct responses. Teacher directs one child to draw a picture to show how the peddler looked when he was selling his caps. Students respond. Teacher asks another student to draw a picture in box 2, showing how the peddler looked when he sat under the tree to rest.

Teacher asks a different student to draw a picture showing how the peddler looked when he discovered that his caps were gone. Then, in box 4, the teacher asks the fourth child to draw pictures showing how the peddler looked when the monkeys wouldn't give him back his caps. Students respond.

The teacher then asks the children to choose a partner and discuss another name they would give the peddler. Each team shares the name they chose with the group. The teacher monitors the activities.

The teacher asks the students the following questions and has them do the following activity:

1. Draw a picture to show how you look when you get angry.
2. Do peddlers or people who sell things come to your house?
3. What are some of the things they sell?
4. Where would you go to buy a cap?
5. What does a peddler do?

XII. ASSESSMENT

- Writing Samples
- READ and RETELL
- Observations
- Student's Observations
- Portfolio
- Journals

LESSON PLAN SAMPLES

STORY MAP

In the country a long time ago

Setting

The monkeys took the peddler's caps when he went to sleep

Problem

Our Story Map for *Caps for Sale*

by: Esphyr Stobodking

Main Characters

Peddler
Monkeys

Solution

The peddler got mad and threw his caps down. All of the monkeys imitated what he did.

Directions:

The teacher discusses the four components of the story with the children and summarizes their responses in the circles.

Caps for Sale   Name _____

Story Structure: Plot Sequence

What Happened Next?

Complete the sentences to tell what happens in the story.

First, the man shook his finger.

Then the monkeys _____

Next, the man shook his hands.

Then the monkeys _____

After that, the man stamped his feet.

Then the monkeys _____

At last, the man _____

At last, the monkeys _____

Reading

CAPS FOR SALE

Make sentence strips as shown. For the words caps and monkeys, draw picture cards. Read the first two sentences aloud. Then have children read them with you as you point to the pictures and words. Repeat the activity a few times, encouraging the children to sound like a peddler. Follow the same procedure for the last two sentences. Point out that the peddler's words changed slightly as he grew angrier. Reread the sentences, adding the words *better* or *must* before the word *give*. Have students try to sound angrier each time.

Picture	!	Picture	for sale	Fifty cents a	Picture	!
You	Picture	you!	You	give me back my		!

better

must

Caps for Sale

HOMEWORK

MAKE SILLY MONKEY PUPPETS

Students can make their own monkeys to act out the story in cooperative learning groups. Or, students may wish to perform a puppet story for parents or for another class.

You need:

> Scissors, cardboard tube (toilet paper-size), paste, crayons or markers, colored construction paper.

CUTOUTS

Steps:
1. Reproduce all the monkey parts and cap once for each child.
2. Have children color the parts and cap and then cut them out. Ask the children to use markers and draw features on the monkey's face.
3. Have the children cut and paste colored construction paper onto the tubes as shown to make each monkey's body.
4. Help children paste the monkey parts and cap onto each body as shown.

MY HAT

Design a hat yourself!

1. Decorate your hat using previously given patterns.
2. Color your hat.
3. Share your hat with the class and tell where you could wear it.

HAT DECORATIONS

Draw Your Favorite Hat

Chapter 10

The Development of Motives and Values in the Child

THEORIES OF CHILD REARING are frequently divorced from theories about the nature of man. Professor Berkowitz's latest findings regarding cultural, religious, social class, and familial influences on the development of morality and the motivation of achievement assesses the theories of socialization in respect of relevant research. Leonard Berkowitz, professor of psychology at the University of Wisconsin, is also author of *Aggression: A Social-Psychological Analysis*.

PIAGET'S ANALYSIS. The eminent Swiss psychologist Jean Piaget has provided what is undoubtedly the most famous description of the development of moral judgment in children. Explicitly recognizing that they were investigating judgments and not behavior, Piaget and his collaborators questioned children "from the poorer parts of Geneva" about certain problematical situations. The children's answers suggested to Piaget that there were two major stages in the formation of moral judgments: The first of these, lasting until 7 or 8 years of age, involves "the morality of constraint"; the second stage is "the morality of cooperation."

In the first stage, supposedly because the child regards adults as dominant and omnipotent, eternal and unchanging rules (which the child believes are handed down by adults) are to be accepted automatically and without question. Children also evaluate behavior in terms of objective consequences, following what Piaget called "the principle of moral realism." As an illustration of this important principle, consider two (paraphrased) hypothetical situations employed by the investigators.

1) A little boy, John, is called to dinner. Unknown to John, behind the door to the dining room is a chair on which is a tray holding 15 cups. As he enters the room, the door knocks against the tray, and all the cups are broken.

2) One day, a little boy named Henry tried to get some jam out of a cupboard when his mother was away from the house. He climbed on a chair, but he could not reach it. While he was trying, however, he knocked over a cup, which broke.

Using moral realism, the younger Swiss children indicated that John was naughtier than Henry. He had broken 15 cups whereas Henry had broken only one.

Justice is often thought at this age to be "immanent," automatically emanating from the objects in the situation. Thus, when hearing of a little child who, contrary to his teacher's orders, had tried to sharpen his pencil with a knife and had cut himself, the youngsters thought that the cut was a punishment arising from the knife itself. They believed that the child would not have cut himself if he had been allowed to use the knife. If punishment has to be administered, it is an expiration. The evildoer must be made to realize the seriousness of his wicked action. The more severe the punishment, then the better or fairer it is.

For example, according to Piaget, when a young child is told of a boy who broke a toy belonging to his little brother, he is likely to advocate expiatory punishment. Given a variety of punishments which might be administered, the youngster typically says that the boy should not be allowed to play with his own toys for a week.

The more mature type of morality, "the morality of cooperation, or reciprocity," generally begins around 9 or 10 years of age. The child's unilateral respect for the dominant, omnipotent adult has given way to mutual respect, cooperation, and increased autonomy for the child. Presumably as a consequence of this change, rules are now no longer regarded as fixed, externally imposed laws. The child now realizes that rules can be altered; they are not coercive, but are based on cooperation and mutual respect. His evaluation of other people's behavior reflects this change, and he considers intention ("subjective responsibility"), rather than objective consequence.

This change can be seen in the responses to the stories about the broken cups. Henry is now labeled the naughtier boy because he had intended to commit a "bad" act. Furthermore, instead of advocating retributive justice, the now-autonomous child, thinking in terms of equality, supposedly, believes that punishment should follow the principle of reciprocity. Punishment should put things right, or restore the status quo ante: Inflicting pain in retribution is not necessary. Thus, on hearing the story of the boy who had broken his little brother's toy, the older children typically called for either reciprocation, the boy should give the brother one of his own toys, or restitution, and he should pay to have it repaired.

According to Piaget, another type of judgment in which there is a consideration of equity begins to emerge at around 11 or 12 years. The child now becomes concerned with the details of the situation he is judging. Taking circumstances into account, he might now forgive certain transgressions. If he were younger, he would be more inclined to believe that the moral violation should be punished in some way merely because it is a violation. But his thought processes have changed with age, and he can now understand and forgive.

Piaget believed that the developmental sequence he described arose from a combination of environmental and maturational events. Adult constraint generally weakens as the child grows older, and much of the older child's altered way of thinking is, as we have seen, supposedly a consequence of his newfound autonomy and self-respect. But the child has also simply grown older, and his increased maturity, presumably, also contributes to his more sophisticated moral judgments.

Empirical investigations carried out in both Europe and the United States in the past 30 years or so have yielded only uneven support for Piaget's analysis. There may well be some age differences in moral judgment, but these judgments clearly are strongly influenced by sociocultural learning. The changes that do take place with increased age are not necessarily products of an automatic maturational process. Equally important, where Piaget regarded moral judgments as forming a unitary pattern in a given developmental stage, later research indicates that there are different and independent forms of judgment even at the same age level.

In one typical investigation, the psychologists interviewed children between 6 and 12 years of age using Piaget's method. Many of the youngsters below 9 years, they found, displayed moral realism in response to the story of the broken cups. In contrast, the majority of the children over 9 considered subjective responsibility (intent), rather than objective consequences. The older group defined naughtiness in terms of the boy's intention and not in terms of the magnitude of the damage he had created.

Nevertheless, the moral judgments made by older children do not always conform to Piaget's analysis. Increased age does not necessarily bring a greater advocacy of reciprocity. Punishment is the physical aggression for having violated property and personal rights.

Contrary to Piaget's observations, older boys and girls are not always ready to insist that "it is strictly fair to give back the blows that one has received." They sometimes believe, for example, that teachers or other authorities are the appropriate people to punish a child who fights, rather than they themselves, and consequently, it is not necessary or right to give back blow for blow.

One of the first investigations of the validity of Piaget's notions indicated that children's moral judgments are affected by both their national culture and their socioeconomic background. Recall that the Swiss psychologist had studied mostly poor children. However, an English psychologist selected a comparable sample of youngsters from the poorer parts of London and a group of children from well-to-do English homes. She found that there was a decrease in moral realism with age only in the lower-class group. The children from the more prosperous families, by contrast, tended to show relatively mature judgment, even at the youngest ages (below 6 years), and the percentage of such evaluations remained fairly constant over the age range.

The findings obtained by this English psychologist appear to be fairly general. Other investigators have also found national and social class differences in moral judgment. Several researchers have also observed differences in moral judgment dependent on social class similar to those reported by Harrow.

Why do we find such cultural and class differences? Bronfenbrenner has hypothesized that authoritarian and arbitrary practices of child rearing as employed by European parents, especially when dealing with their very young children, were largely responsible for the two-stage sequence observed by Piaget. The young European child was typically completely dominated by his mother and father and thus, could have easily adopted the morality of constraint. It was not until he was older, Bronfenbrenner suggested, that he was treated in a more rational, egalitarian manner. Consistent with this reasoning, parents taking extreme points of view regarding child rearing, as is likely to be the case in authoritarian families, tend to have children who exhibit immature moral judgment, especially in the areas of immanent justice and the belief in the efficacy of extreme punishment.

A Child's Experiences in a Particular Religious Culture

The Catholic Church, for example, regards 7 years as the age of reason. A 7-year-old Catholic child must learn the difference between accidents and sinful actions so that he knows what must, and what need not, be confessed. Whether some behavior is sinful frequently depends, of course, on the intent of the action, and consequently, young Catholic children are taught to evaluate a deed for its motivation.

Not surprisingly, then, Catholic parochial schoolchildren have been found to give mature responses to Piaget-type stories at an earlier age than public school children regardless of the social class or intelligence level of the children. The Catholic youngsters had learned to consider subjective responsibility because this learning was important in their religion.

Differences in learning conditions can also account for the differences in judgment displayed by middle- and working-class children. As a result, working-class youngsters are more likely than their middle-class peers to evaluate an act in terms of its consequences, rather than of its intent. This difference corresponds to differences in the major concerns of their parents.

Interviews with a sample of white working-class families in Washington, D.C., indicated that the working-class parents gave greater attention to the surface appearances of their children's actions. They evidently wanted qualities in their children that would assure respectability. Respectability could easily be endangered or lost altogether if their children violated social prescriptions. Above all, their children had to avoid the open display of antisocial acts.

The middle-class parents, by contrast, were much more secure in their social status. They did not fear actions that would undermine a precarious social position, and they could, therefore, go beyond appearance. They wanted their children to develop the appropriate internal standards by which they could regulate their own behavior, and so, they generally considered a child's motives when evaluating his behavior. There is little wonder, then, that middle-class boys and girls are also relatively prone to take subjective responsibility into account in making moral judgments. They learn to copy their parents.

Parents shape the nature of their children's moral judgments in several ways. As we have just seen, they may serve as models for their young children, or they may even explicitly teach their offspring to evaluate certain situations in a given manner. In addition, parents may also establish a type of home in which only particular forms of moral evaluations can develop.

Parents holding extreme attitudes regarding child-rearing practices also tend to have children who are immature in some aspects of their moral judgments. What is probably more important, family life can also determine whether a child evaluates immoral behavior in terms of his own internal standards of right and wrong or only considers the possibility of being caught and punished.

According to one study, those youngsters who think mainly of whether the immoral act will be detected and punished typically see their parents as being punitively assertive and controlling. Growing up with harsh, punitive, and demanding parents, they apparently have not formed strong moral standards of their own for evaluating the propriety of a given action.

Differences in Parental Disciplinary Techniques

This also contributes to the class differences in moral judgment. On the average, middle-class and working-class mothers and fathers do not discipline their children in the same manner. The middle-class parent is more likely to be moderate, if not lenient. He will overlook some offenses that his working-class counterpart will typically punish.

If he does exert discipline, he is more inclined to try to reason with his child or even make him feel guilty for his misdeed.

Probably reflecting these child-rearing differences, more children from the middle than from the lower socioeconomic levels look behind a youngster's immediate misdeed. Instead of prescribing punishment, a middle-class child is more prone than his working-class peers to suggest that the young culprit's environment may have to be changed. He realizes that environmental features may have produced the immoral action. If the middle-class child does advocate some form of punishment, in contrast to the working-class youngsters, he is less likely to call for personal punishment of the naughty child.

Again the lesson is clear. Whether the child just copies his parents, learns to make those judgments that will gain approval from them, or develops those moral values that help him cope with a restrictive and frustrating home, his learning experiences play a more important role than do his maturational processes in forming his moral judgments.

Bandura and McDonald have reported a direct demonstration of how parental influences can modify children's moral judgments. Five-to-eleven-year-old children first indicated their judgments of a wide variety of verbally described social situations, as in the Piaget procedure, and then, sometime later, were divided into three experimental groups. In two of these conditions, the child observed an adult (actually the experimenter's confederate) express moral judgment about similar stories. The adults' judgments went counter to the child's initial orientation and were approved by the experimenter.

In one of the experimental groups, the child was also given approval by the experimenter whenever he adopted the adult's mode of making judgments during this second phase, whereas in the second condition, he was not so reinforced for expressing evaluations deviating from his initial beliefs. The children in the third condition were not provided with an adult model, but were given approval for making evaluations that differed from their initial judgments.

Finally, as a test of the extent to which learning had occurred, each child was then taken to another room where a second experimenter asked him to offer judgments in response to a series of additional stories without the adult being present. (We might note here that, in making the moral judgments, the child had to define "naughtiness" in terms of either objective consequences or subjective responsibility.)

In general, the researchers found the child was most likely to have altered his initial type of evaluation when he had seen the adult being given approval for expressing these differing judgments. It mattered little whether the child had also been given approval. Furthermore, there was virtually no change in those children who had been given the social rewards without an adult being present.

The children had clearly adopted the types of judgment verbalized by the reinforced adult model. Learning experiences, especially those in which parents and other significant adults have a major role, contribute a great deal to the exact nature of the child's moral judgments. We assume that the adequately socialized child should evaluate ethical situations in particular ways.

Most clinically oriented social workers, psychologists, and psychiatrists realize that moral behavior as well as moral judgments depend on the formation of strong consciences. The development of conscience or (to use the psychoanalytic concept of) the superego presumably eliminates the necessity of constant surveillance and threats of punishment.

When the child is very young, the child must be controlled by direct parental action. The mother must prevent her child from touching the hot stove or the sharp knife and keep him from wandering out into the street because he is too young to understand the dangers involved in such situations.

As he gets older, he learns that his parents want him to do certain things at certain times and not to do other things. He gets approval for carrying out the desired actions and some form of punishment if he departs from his parents' standards. With time and continued learning, he comes to control himself.

This type of self-control is, however, ultimately based on the anticipation of detection. The child carries out the desired action or avoids the prohibited behavior because he believes that the people who can reward or punish him will find out what he has done. It is not until he has truly internalized parental and social moral standards that he will behave in a socially proper fashion solely because this is the "right" thing to do. He now supposedly has a strong conscience, an adequately developed superego. He can be trusted to behave in a socially appropriate manner without external threats. If he fails to act properly, he will feel guilty, and he presumably wants to avoid the arousal of guilt.

This section examines research bearing on this common conception. Three major points are made: (1) For many people in our society, inner controls are not sufficient to inhibit socially disapproved behavior. These inner controls evidently have to be reinforced by the actions of other people. (2) The conscience should not be regarded as a unitary, ever-active internal agency of the personality. (3) Parents play an active part in the development of internal standards of conduct.

It is my belief that all of the school administrators are trained adequately, and they can also serve as consultants working directly with the staff in their school districts creating staff development models that support research-based instruction. They will then become a team of collaborators working together and being knowledgeable of the mission statement that would empower all students with academic skills, knowledge, and confidence to become productive members of society. They will also establish an atmosphere that promotes positive personal interaction, responsibility, accountability, and self-discipline among students and district staff along with teachers. In-service training will ensure that a positive learning environment and high expectations are maintained at all schools, enabling all students to attain academic success.

Clinical Child Psychology

I agree with the major goal stated in the second paragraph of the article concerning clinical child psychology which states that the program provides a richness of learning experiences from which children can choose, in a setting which is constructed to reward self-initiated activities, where the teachers work toward this goal by viewing themselves as one of the many experiences available to children.

I do believe that it is the duty and responsibility for all teachers to be visible, making themselves available to students as role models of skills and strategies that help students to practice and apply the modeled strategies in becoming independent learners.

I also agree with the statement in the article that describes one of the teacher's tasks, that is, to critically observe the children and then accurately assess their needs.

I have followed the guidelines of the assessment section of Open Court which states that continuous assessment enables teachers to gauge the progress of their students so that no student misses needed instruction. The assessment of Open Court contains:

- Program Assessment
- Teacher's Observation Log
- Pretest
- Midyear test
- Posttest

Open Court also includes assessments for all skills taught in the unit. In my experience as a teacher in the classroom for kindergarten students, along with colleagues to improve professional practice, we developed a monthly grade level assessment result chart, which included all subject areas across the curriculum. (See kindergarten assessments and monthly grade level assessment result charts in observational tools))

We worked together in establishing and communicating learning goals for all students based on the California Standards for the teaching profession and the Open Court Reading Instructional Plan across the curriculum aligned with the school districts' Language Arts: Reading, Writing, Listening, and Speaking activities based on Academic Content Standards. The results of assessments helped us to use multiple sources of information to communicate with administrators, students, and families about student progress. We also established and communicated learning goals for all students and guided them in assessing their own learning, giving them opportunities to assist in individualizing instruction.

Chapter 11

Ethnic Diversity and Contemporary Families

MY PERSONAL FEELINGS ABOUT ETHNIC diversity and contemporary families in America today does not center on the melting pot theory, based on scientific study and research with many different ethnic groups of immigrants that have emigrated from other countries.

I do not think ethnic identity should be the central theme in America on how family systems are organized and how families are structured. I do think that ethnic identity should continue to be the factor that influences their motives and values according to Staples and Mirande, stated in the article.

It is my belief that we Americans lack the information that is needed to make reliable generalizations about cultural differences in development. When we compare differences in child-rearing practices and conditions, we find differences in intellectual ability relating to early learning and sociocultural differences.

I agree with the research in the article that many minority families today still struggle with prejudices and discrimination that limits educational experiences, job opportunities, and the ability to function fully in communities.

However, in public schools, where most of the children of immigrants attend schools, especially beginning in grade school, kindergarten students are taught standards in history and social science to empower all students with academic skills, knowledge, confidence, and the commitment to pursue lifelong learning and to become productive members of society.

They are taught to understand that being a good citizen involves acting in a certain way following rules, such as sharing and taking turns, and understand the consequences of breaking them. They are taught examples of honesty, determination, individual responsibility, and patriotism in America and world history from stories and folklore.

All students are taught to understand that history relates to events, people, and places of the present, past, and future. They are also taught to identify the purposes of, and the people and events honored in commemorative holidays, including the human struggles that were the basis for the events (e.g., Thanksgiving, Independence Day, Washington's and Lincoln's Birthdays, Martin Luther King, Jr., Day, Memorial Day, Labor Day, and Columbus Day).

Children eventually learn the triumphs in American legends and historical accounts through the stories of such people as Pocahontas, George Washington Carver, Booker T. Washington, Daniel Boone, and Benjamin Franklin.

Students are also taught to understand how people lived in earlier times and how their lives would be different today (e.g., drawing water from a well, growing food, making clothing, having fun, forming organizations, and living by rules and law).

Chapter 12

The Future of Learning into the Twenty-First Century

"THE FUTURE OF LEARNING INTO the Twenty-First Century" has been excerpted from a paper prepared for the White House Conference on Children by a group headed by Dr. John I. Goodlad, dean of the Graduate School of Education at the University of California, Los Angeles.

Rationale

Educational change is desperately needed because so many people in this country have been denied the right to learn. Among the many reasons for this denial, one stands out—our mindless adherence to unproductive teaching concepts and practices. Change is absolutely essential.

Preservice training and in-service development of teachers in an age of scientific acceleration and technological advance presents complex problems for educators. The obsolescence of skills, knowledge, and competencies in teaching dictates the need for continuous staff development. Recent technological advancements have sharpened the awareness of and the need for educational innovations that contribute to effective teaching.

Objectives:

Teachers should be able to:

1. develop a case in support of the need for educational change
2. defend the viewpoint that education of the future will feature learning, not as a means to some end, but rather as an end itself
3. outline the role of instructional technology in realizing the goals of education in the twenty-first century
4. contrast education as it exists today with your conception of education in the future
5. give evidence of a favorable attitude toward educational change as a concept and as a goal to strive for by listing specific changes you would adopt in your own area of responsibility

In a nation that speaks of inalienable rights, the right to learn must be paramount. Yet, that right, in its full meaning, has been denied to many in this nation. It has been denied because of color, religion, poverty, infirmity, and residence.

The right to learn is the goal we seek for the twenty-first century. We want for our children a range of learning opportunities as broad as the unknown range of their talents: We want a learning environment that nurtures those talents. We want our children to know themselves and be secure in that knowledge to open themselves to others. We want them to have freedom, and justice, and peace that the preservation of freedom demands.

Black and brown, yellow and red cultures, we have too often ignored and implicitly denigrated other cultures at an inestimable cost to all our children.

The full extent of the denial of the right to learn is even greater, however, for we tend to paint only pretty pictures of life out of differences supposedly to the tenderness of children. In so doing, we magnify our hypocrisy for all to see. Even the youngest of our offspring soon become aware that we wage war while talking peace, that children go hungry in the richest land on the face of the earth, that even leaders cheat and lie. They come to understand that what we say and what we do are very different things. They see with the uncluttered vision of children the gap between rhetoric and reality.

What is to be learned is refined by our filtering system, until, too often, it has little power to grip the learner and, thus, defrauds or cheats him. From the truly exciting possibilities of a culture—or conscience—embracing mankind, we slide to the homogenized "adventures" of Dick and Jane and a field trip to the supermarket.

With regard to the "how" of learning, we have only begun to question the outworn notion that certain subjects or concepts are to be learned by all individuals at successive stages of growth, at stipulated times, in sterile places. Reading is for the first grade, long division for the fourth, and fractions for the fifth and sixth. All of this takes place between the hours of nine and three in a big box divided into cells. Preschool prepares for adjustment to the next-larger box.

In this lockstep, as in so many other ways, we teach that each phase of life is instrumental to the next rather than of ultimate value in itself. We see the man we want the child to become, rather than the child seeking to become himself. In the words of Hannah Arendt, "Man sees wood in every tree."

Toward Better Schools

Until recently, we believed that we had only to provide some new subject matter here, inject a heavier dose of phonics there, or tighten the discipline a little, to improve both the system and society. Better schools (defined in largely quantitative terms) would mean more jobs, a brisker economy, larger cities, and more aware, dedicated citizens. *Or so we thought.* Dwindling confidence in these relationships reflects both declining public confidence in the schools and the tenacity with which we cling to the "learning equals school" equation.

Painfully, we are coming to realize that grades predict grades, that success in school begets success in more schools but is no guarantee of good workers, committed citizens, happy mothers and fathers, or compassionate human beings.

Whereas for many years they fulfilled brilliantly the primary purpose for which they were founded—the creation of one nation out of millions of immigrants, recent decades brought them new kinds of clientele whose needs could not be met with the formulas and procedures that had been used previously.

For a brief span of years, we believed that serious problems existed only in the schools of our great cities. The failures of our schools are apparent in dropout rates, in barely minimal learning on the part of many who do remain in school, and in growing alienation among the young of all colors and classes.

At the root of the problem is an implicit denial of diversity. The schools have become great sorting machines, labeling and certifying those who presumably will be winners and losers as adults. The winners are disproportionately white and affluent. The losers, too often, are poor and brown or black or red.

But many of the winners are losers too. For they are shaped, directed, and judged according to a narrow conception of what is right and proper. This process begins very early. The environment of expectations, rewards, and punishments is established before mother and child leave the hospital. And in the home, infants are encouraged in their efforts to walk and talk, but their responses to sound, color, and smell are ignored or stifled.

This process of channeling energy and talent is refined and perfected in the schools through a network of expectations, rules, grades, required subjects, and rewards for what is wanted and the subtle extinction of the great range of talents and achievements which are not wanted.

A massive task of change lies ahead. We cannot point with pride at those who have "made it" while half of us believe that life has passed us by. We cannot rejoice with our sons and daughters when their brothers and sisters do not graduate with them. We cannot congratulate ourselves on our talents when half of our talents have withered or died.

The inflated rhetoric we have used in describing our accomplishments far exceeds their nature and extent. Among many of our people there is a sense of outrage induced by the discrepancy between what is said and what could be. Thankfully, however, not all our energies are used up in anger. We have more than a little hope that a new era can be both described and created. At the core of this hope is a fresh awareness of children: of their intrinsic rather than instrumental value, of their ability to learn, and of the kind of learning they could and should have as we look to the twenty-first century.

Other generations believed that they had the luxury of preparing their children to live in a society similar to their own. The primary—although seldom attained—aim of education was thus to transmit the existing culture to the young. Ours is the first generation to have achieved the Socratic wisdom of knowing that we did not know the world of the year 2000, in which our children lived.

To speak, as we have in the past, of giving our young the "tools" with which to survive, to speak of techniques and "subjects" as the essential components of education is important to send our children, well equipped, toward learning in the twentieth-first century.

All that we can predict with certainty is that the central issue of the twenty-first century will be the struggle to assert truly human values and to achieve their ascendancy in a highly technological society. It will be the struggle to place man in a healthy relationship with his natural environment; to place him in command of, rather than subservient to, the wondrous technology he is creating; and to give him the breadth and depth of understanding which can result in the formation of a world culture, embracing and nurturing within its transcending characteristics the diverse cultures of today's world.

We ask first then, not what kind of education we want to provide, but what kind of human being we want to emerge. What would we have the twenty-first-century man be?

We would have him be a man with a strong sense of himself and his own humanness, with awareness of his thoughts and feelings, with the capacity to feel and express love and joy, and to recognize tragedy and feel grief.

We would have him be a man who, with a strong and realistic sense of his own worth, is able to relate openly with others, to cooperate effectively with them toward common ends, and to view mankind as one while respecting diversity and difference.

We would want him to be a being who, even while very young, somehow senses that he has it within himself to become more than he now is, that he has the capacity for lifelong spiritual and intellectual growth.

We would want him to cherish that vision of the man he is capable of becoming and to cherish the development of the same potentiality in others.

The education of this kind of human being is necessarily an enabling process rather than an instructional process. It requires opening the whole of the world to the learner and giving him easy access to that world. This implies enormous respect for the child's capacity to learn, and with the granting of respect goes, by implication, the granting of freedom.

In the year 2000, we see learning not as a means to some end but as an end in itself. Education will not be an imitation of life but life examined and enjoyed. A prescribed age for beginning to learn—or for ceasing to learn—will be meaningless. So will age as a criterion for determining what needs to be learned. And so will the standard school day and the standard academic year.

Compulsory education—or compulsory attendance, as it might better be called—will be a thing of the past. School as we know it will have been replaced by a diffused learning involvement involving homes, parks, public buildings, museums, business offices, and guidance centers. Many such resources that are now unendorsed, unofficial, unrecognized, unstructured, or unsupervised—and unused—will be endorsed and made fully available for learning. There will be successors to our present schools, places designed for people to gather for purposes of learning things together.

The mere availability of a broad range of options will signify what we believe will be an important, and essential, change in our national value system. The word success will have been redefined, and a far wider range of choices—of study, of taste, of career, of "lifestyle"—will be legitimized and seen as praiseworthy.

Modern technology will help us realize our goals. The profound significance of the computer, when properly used in learning, is that it introduces an entirely new source of energy into the educational process. Subjects missed this year can be picked up next year.

The 50-year-old need not humble himself by going back to school with 12-year-olds to get what he wants. He may go directly to the energy system, which is not aware of age, color, place, birth, or time of day.

It is possible that advanced technology will return the family to the center of the stage as the basic learning unit. Each home could become a school, in effect, via an electronic console connected to a central computer system, a videotape and microfilm library regulated by a computer, and a national educational television network. Whether at home or elsewhere, each student of whatever age will have at the touch of a button access to a comprehensive "learning package," including printed lessons, experiments to be performed, recorded information, videotaped lectures, and films.

Excellence in Teacher Preparation

I like the concept of Professional Development Schools known as PDS that emerged during the school reform efforts of the 1980s, which was the reform agenda that led to conceptual changes for classrooms, as well as the way teachers were prepared.

I agree with the reform agenda that continued the changes needed in teacher training with a shift in emphasis towards high standards of learning for both students and teachers, providing educational opportunities for pre-kindergarten through 12th-grade students.

It is true that a standard program based on scientific research provides a variety of proven experiences for accommodating individual students' needs. It gives teachers the opportunity to grow professionally and establish professional goals.

It is my belief that teacher training programs should have a primary goal of improving student achievement districtwide along with collaborative efforts of staff, parents, and community members in motivating students to strive for excellence.

I also agree with Clark, who identified in this article four main purposes of the Professional Development Schools which are:

1. To provide a clinical setting for preservice education.
2. To engage in teachers' professional development.

3. To promote and conduct inquiry, and
4. To provide exemplary education for pre-K-12th-grade students.

In order for the four purposes stated by Clark in this article to stretch the teachers' understanding of education, all teachers must get involved in a standard-based program such as SRA Open Court Reading.

I have worked with kindergarten students using this program and found it to be very successful for teaching students to read and write with skill and confidence. All strategies and skills are arranged from the simplest to the most complex.

The Open Court Reading provides more comprehensive Teacher Editions than any other program. The presentation of concepts, skills, and practice is detailed. All teachers need to do is follow the directions.

Finally, The U.S. Department of Education's Reading Excellence Act has awarded state grants to improve reading achievement, mandating that schools choose programs that show scientifically based research and effective practices that have been replicated effectively. Open Court has been the program of choice for schools throughout the nation who are being awarded this grant.

Learning to Teach in Urban Settings

I agree with Gay and the statement which said, teacher candidates need an understanding of urban cultures, as well as the pedagogy and skills that will help them implement a meaningful curriculum for urban students.

It is widely known that teacher education programs throughout the United States are searching for ways in how to raise the achievement levels of children in diverse settings.

In my experience as a teacher working in public school settings, especially in early childhood, I have been greatly influenced by developmentalists, as they have tried to respond to the diverse needs of individual children. I have learned that their greatest concern is planning and implementing developmentally appropriate curriculum that will address the needs of all students. Therefore, the challenge is to reconstruct the selection procedures for curriculum, pedagogy, and assessment in ways that better address the knowledge, skills, practices, and aspirations of the children at risk. In order to do this, we must consider children's diverse cultural backgrounds and understand the challenges of teaching and what it means to teach in urban settings.

I also agree with the statement by Villegas and Lucas that teachers need to be more cognizant of the fact that a commitment to teach in urban settings goes beyond knowledge about the curriculum and how children learn. It touches a much-deeper issue which is how to connect the curriculum to children's everyday lives.

I believe that the theory of culture identity takes the position that some children have a deep sense of belonging to, or being connected with, culture. This becomes particularly problematic because people often identify with a culture based on class, gender, ethnicity, and religion. Teachers must resist the temptation to stereotype children. They must act as cultural mediators, helping children to feel comfortable with their own identities within the school context.

I also believe that children should not feel that they have to choose between their own success and their cultural identity. It is the teacher's responsibility to create an environment in which children's abilities and values are recognized, then the children won't adopt patterns of resistance to the authority of teachers and schools, which they will perceive as a pervasive constraint on their feelings of well-being.

I believe the time has come that teachers should respond in a positive way to the challenges presented in this article, "Learning to Teach in

Urban Settings." They need to recognize their responsibilities to work with the children's strengths and knowledge to help them to achieve success in the school culture.

Finally, in order to move closer to significantly equal, fair, developmentally meaningful, as well as culturally congruent curriculum for young children's learning experiences, teachers must realize the contemporary cultural complexities in young children's lives. They need to start at their personal level of learning in early childhood. Educators should be aware of the complexities they encounter and strive to understand how the cultural complexities can affect the knowledge of subject matter, content, and student development.

Also, teachers must respond to the challenges presented in this article and provide a literacy learning environment that is fair, enabling, and effective, and that will ensure equality and success for all students to achieve through the collaborative efforts of teachers, parents, and community motivating students to strive for excellence.

Chapter 13

Learn English as a Second Language

I AGREE WITH VYGOTSKY REGARDING play and language learning. He states that children are naturally able to learn many things by interacting with their parents, caregivers, adults, and peers through play, no matter what language they speak.

I believe that parents are the central contributors to a child's education, especially in preschool programs, and interacting with their own child is the key to their child's success.

In order for a program to work successfully, schools must work successfully, schools must work cooperatively with all parents. Schools must recognize the value diversity and difficulty of parents interacting with their own children at times.

I also believe that all parents have hopes and goals for their children.

I agree with the Vygotsky regarding play as a leading activity for promoting a child's development, stating that play also serves many functions in nurturing their cognitive, social, emotional, and linguistic development.

I think teachers should create a physical environment that engages all students in learning through play. Since play is important in helping to prepare preschool children for kindergarten, it is necessary for teachers to plan activities in the classroom where teachers could observe the children's interest at play. The same activity could be repeated day after day to increase a child's experience and involvement and to target other specific skills, such as learning interpersonal skills that increase their ability to function successfully as members of a group.

I also agree with Avgitidou, Jason, and Miller. They stated that children can find socially acceptable ways of fulfilling their needs and also enhance their feelings of self-esteem and competence.

I do believe that students learn when curriculum is relevant to their lives, when it is of personal interest to them, and when they are actively engaged in the pursuit of knowledge.

In my opinion, dramatic play is a good example for children to articulate the many cognitive, social, emotional, and physical developmental accomplishments of the curriculum.

Teachers should set up a dramatic play area with clothing that identifies the role of the person. Among the favorite role models of preschool children are policeman, fireman, doctor, nurse, parents. These activities should provide children with the opportunities to creatively express themselves and demonstrate their knowledge of each individual's responsibility.

Also, teachers should engage students in problem solving, critical thinking, and other activities that make subject matter meaningful. These concepts of readiness should focus on the child's development, learning, as well as physical, social, and emotional skills. They also include cognitive skills that promote group responsibility, which, in turn, facilitates learning experiences that promote autonomy, interaction, and individual choice.

Chapter 14

Effective Practices and Principles to Support English Language Learners in the Early Childhood Classroom

I AGREE WITH THIS ARTICLE that states in the very first paragraph that in the United States, early childhood teachers must balance diverse needs in their classrooms and often must modify instruction for students who are learning English as a new language.

I believe that effective practices for English language learners in the early childhood classroom are addressed in the Open Court Reading Program that adheres to California State Standards that align with California Reading/Language Arts requirements.

The English Language Development lessons address the needs of today's increasingly diverse classrooms. This instructional support complements the Open Court Reading lessons. Also, Home Connections Blackline Masters include parent letters in both Spanish and English to communicate classroom progress, including unit themes and activities.

Open Court is available for students ranging from Pre-K to 6th grade. The diverse ethnic and cultural makeup of today's classrooms makes it unlikely that one single curriculum will meet the needs and interests of all students. Curriculum must be flexible so that teachers are able to construct lessons that will be of high interest to their unique group of students, and actively engage them in creating knowledge. Teachers should use a variety of instructional strategies and resources to respond to students' diverse needs.

Chapter 15

"The Culture of Teaching"

Guest Editors, Lauren Ventimiglia and Thomas Reed

THE CULTURE OF TEACHING continues to evolve with changing times, but the need for high-quality educators remains a constant. One of the greatest challenges educators face today is training future educators in a highly supportive and facilitative environment. The paradox of teacher education and student learning is that there are many differing criteria among teacher education programs, states, and local school districts. The coursework, field experiences, and mentorship requirements also vary tremendously. Additionally, state standards and high-stakes testing contribute to the many discrepancies.

The debate continually rages over whether education should focus on current politics and mandated, financially supported programs or on the cultivation of innovative teaching methods.

Early childhood and elementary education continue to be influenced by these various factors. The field of education is intrinsically diverse, both economically and geographically. As a result of this diversification, educators have much to glean from one another, yet teacher education varies drastically from one institution to another. Once they enter the workforce, novice teachers are expected to perform to district standards, with or without the help of mentors. Furthermore, mentorship programs vary greatly—certain districts provide appropriate training while many others fail to provide training or even mentors.

A persistent and deep-rooted incongruency exists among perspectives regarding educators as professionals. Educators, who are trained and certified, view themselves as professionals, yet they are seldom accorded the respect commonly given to those in other professions.

Finally, more culturally responsive teachers are necessary to provide authentic instruction for increasingly diversified communities. Teachers vary greatly in style as well as delivery and instruction. This factor should be embraced and utilized as a tool within educational systems.

The estimated turnover rate for novice teachers is one-third during the first year. A much more startling statistic is that nearly 50 percent of teachers leave the profession within their first 5 years (Hunt and Carroll, 2003). This issue of *Childhood Education* addresses all these circumstances and concerns and provides both meaningful insight and practical methods to support the continuously changing culture of teaching.

"The Culture of Teaching" theme originated at the annual ACEI Publications Committee meeting in January 2002. It generated overwhelming response and support from the committee members who agreed that many current problems of education lie within differing perspectives on how to train and mentor preservice teachers. The collaboration of educators can bridge the gap between teacher education, novice teachers, mentors, administrators, and educational frameworks.

As coeditors, we invited members of the education community at large to address these underlying issues as well as to formulate a framework of ideas to assimilate into current educational practices. The articles in this issue have a common thread: each one focuses on issues related to educating, attaining, mentoring, and retaining high-quality teachers who will be willing and able to perform in diverse settings.

"Excellence in Teacher Preparation: Partners for Success," coauthored by Laura McDonald Hooks and Linda Randolph, discusses an innovative teaching training program that involves professional development schools (PDS). This article reviews a unique university collaboration with a PDS and the development of a partnership between a university and a child development center. It considers student reports and reflections on the partnership's impact. Moreover, the authors examine the impact of the relationship on preservice teachers after graduation and find a highly positive correlation.

The PDS is organized to support exemplary student and preservice teacher education, with a true collaboration among educators and colleagues, as well as accountability for quality teaching and learning. This true collaboration includes staff, faculty, administrators, and parents, and facilitates higher quality training for preservice teachers and better overall preparation compared to the customary student teaching experience.

Tata Mbugua, professor of teacher education at the University of Scranton, Pennsylvania, and coauthors Jean Wadas, Mary Ann Casey, and Jessica Finnerty, explore preservice training in "Authentic Learning: Intercultural, International, and Intergenerational Experiences in Elementary Classrooms." This article expounds on how the culture of teaching requires both creative and practical initiatives in a given location. A collaborative partnership of preservice teachers, cooperating teachers, and the university supervisor can support and prepare teachers to be culturally responsive through intercultural, international, and intergenerational experiences.

A third article exploring the need for high-quality teacher education is "Learning to Teach in Urban Settings," by Valeria Duarte and Thomas

Reed of the University of South Carolina Spartanburg. Teacher education programs in the United States are attempting to address the need for more culturally responsive teachers to raise the level of achievement in diverse communities.

Statistically, 1 in 3 children are of minority background, yet there is a continuous downward trend in urban achievement levels. Challenges for teachers and students include language barriers, issues associated with poverty, and racial and ethnic differences between students and teachers. Public and private schools find it difficult to attract and retain high-quality teachers.

Believing that preservice teachers need to be more culturally aware and responsive, the authors performed a study that provides meaningful conclusions. They demonstrate the need for a well-designed teacher education program that addresses the need for teaching in culturally diverse settings and leads to better prepared and trained candidates.

As coeditors, we decided to include a narrative of a difficult student teaching experience, which the author aptly titled "Making Lemonade from Lemons: Reflecting on Difficult Experiences." Sue Grossman from Eastern Michigan University offers her personal narrative of a seemingly negative student-teacher experience. Her cooperating teacher focused on control and quiet as a measure of success, which conflicted with the student teacher's enthusiasm and active learning approach.

Grossman overcame the adversity of her experience—a negative classroom learning environment for the students and the student teacher, as well as lack of guidance from her university supervisor—by maintaining idealistic hope. Grossman concludes that the difficulties she endured only heightened her knowledge and success as a teacher. She since has served as a cooperating teacher and as a professor of teacher education.

While this issue examines teacher education in-depth, it also maintains that strong and high-quality mentorship programs need to be implemented for all novice teachers. The Pot of Gold at the End of the Rainbow: Mentoring in Early Childhood Education presents the need for more highly qualified and culturally sensitive mentors in early childhood education.

Lauren Cummins, assistant professor of early childhood teacher education at Youngstown State University, enumerates the various traits required of high-quality mentors. The author includes meaningful assessments to evaluate the impact of this particular mentoring course. She found an enormously positive response from those mentored in areas of efficacy as well as encouragement and self-value. It appears that both the mentor and novice teacher have the ability to grow from this reflective practice.

Paula E. Weaver's submission, "The Culture of Teaching and Mentoring for Compliance," discusses the impact of the No Child Left Behind Act and high-stakes testing and its relationship to the culture of teaching. She demonstrates that the culture of teaching honors children, while standardized testing detracts from the focus of learning. Furthermore, a heightened fixation on testing limits teachers' professional growth opportunities.

Author Lea Lee, assistant professor of education curriculum and instruction at Old Dominion University, Virginia, wrote the "The Culture of Children's Reading in Korea and the United States," which offers a comparison of literacy education in the United States and Korea, and thus, a comparison of the different level of competence that teachers face in the classroom. Many school-age children in the United States read below grade level, which contrasts greatly with corresponding reading levels in Korea.

The author states that four factors contribute to these differences. First, Koreans have a strong belief in academic achievement. Second, Korean parents believe that children should learn a significant amount of knowledge before entering kindergarten. Third, Korean parents believe they have the responsibility of spending considerable time in quasi-formal preschool activities. Finally, Korean parents heed what they feel is their financial obligation to provide children with educational books, tutors, and supplemental materials. The author provides specific examples of a traditional Korean environment with a young child and states that American parents have the ability to provide more support for early literacy and educational support.

Finally, we included a narrative that touches on the art of education: "Teaching From the Heart ... It's About Max and Maureen," written by Lynn E. Nielson, professor of education. This is a personal narrative of how two teachers affected the author's professional life. Max was a nurturing fourth-grade instructor who inspired the author to teach. Maureen was a generous mentor in Neilsen's novice teaching experience. The article explores students and colleagues making connections, and demonstrates how the practice of good teaching comes from the heart, rather than from traditional standards and benchmarks.

Coediting "The Culture of Teaching" has proven to be insightful and rewarding. We were impressed with both the quantity and quality of submissions. More important, we are encouraged by the positive experiences our preservice teachers are getting in many parts of the world. Unfortunately, the emphasis is often placed on what is wrong about education as opposed to what is right and working well.

As coeditors, we represent the two ends of the professional spectrum of education. Lauren Ventimiglia is a fifth-year teacher with a bachelor's degree in both elementary and early childhood education. She has worked for 4 years for the board of education in Wayne, New Jersey, and for one year in a bilingual school in Paris, France.

Tom Reed is a former kindergarten teacher and holds his doctorate in early childhood education; he has participated in the supervisory/mentor role, curriculum development, and teacher education preparation and practice at the University of South Caroline

Spartanburg. Combined, our educational experiences have provided us with a unique perspective on the culture of teaching and mentorship.

We would like to take this opportunity to thank each of our authors as well as acknowledge the continued support of ACEI's Publications Committee. We hope that this compilation of articles provides a meaningful and introspective view on the profession of teaching and training and on the diversity of society. We believe that highly qualified teachers and strong educational institutions, combined with the focus on understanding the culture of teaching and mentorship, provide the key to the future.

Childhood Education
Annual Theme 2004
Reference
Hunt, J. B., and Carroll, T. G. (2003). No dream denied: A pledge to America's children. Washington, D.C.: National Commission on Teaching and America's Future.

The Culture of Teaching

I do not agree with the guest editors Lauren Ventimiglia and Thomas Reed when they said state standards and high-stakes testing contribute to the many discrepancies among teacher education programs, states, and local school districts.

I strongly believe that every public school in all school districts should follow these rules.

1. Provide a Mission Statement
2. Purpose
3. Program goals
4. Program objectives
5. Core curriculum (purpose, goals, and objectives, and state standards)

6. Ongoing assessment
7. Working with communities to improve professional practices
8. Working with families to improve professional practices
9. Working with colleagues to improve professional practices

I do not agree with the editors' statement saying the greatest challenges educators face today is training future educators in a highly supportive and facilitative environment.

Most public schools in the state of California are located in communities where most of the children have grown up in or lived in adjoining communities close by, meaning that many of the parents are able to walk to the schools and give their support as a volunteer. Also, many of the schools provide an enrichment program that involve parents interacting with their own children, which strengthens bonds between home and school, parent and educator, parent and child, school and community.

I do agree with the guest editors Lauren Ventimiglia and Thomas Reed who said that there are many differing criteria among teacher education programs, states, and local school districts. The editors also stated that the debate continually rages over whether education should focus on current politics and mandated, financially supported programs or on the cultivation of innovative teaching methods.

I believe that education should focus on innovated teaching methods because methodology focuses on educational objectives, such as Bloom's Taxonomy, the building blocks of knowledge that extends students' thinking in the areas of the following:

Recall:	Learning the information
Comprehension:	Understanding the information
Application:	Using the information
Analysis:	Examining specific parts of the information

Synthesis:	Doing something new and different with information
Evaluation	Judging the information

I also believe that students should be involved in a literature and critical thinking program to engage them in a discovery process which clarifies thinking, increases knowledge, and deepens their understanding of human issues and social values.

Literature and critical thinking also help teachers to organize curriculum to support student understanding of subject matter and to engage students in problem-solving critical thinking and other activities that make subject matter meaningful.

I also believe that the field of education is intrinsically diverse, both economically and geographically, according to the guest editors, Lauren Ventimiglia and Thomas Reed.

It is true that teachers and administrators, as well as students and communities, are confronted with a range of cultural shifts that include a large number of multicultural and multilingual school populations.

It is our responsibility to create and manage school environments that are fair and effective, that teach in ways that encourage learning to develop a curriculum to ensure strict adherence to California Standards for the teaching profession, along with the school districts Academic Content Standards for grades K–12.

The Culture of Teaching
Native American Indian Parents and Children

I agree with John Yellowbird and Snipp who say that there may be similarities between Native American Indian family systems and those of other minority groups.

I also believe that the most important feature of childhood is the development of an identity. As children shape their behavior and values, they may look to heroes and role models for guidance. They may identify the role models they wish to emulate based on possession of certain skills or attributes. While the child may not want to be exactly like the person, he or she may see possibilities in that person. Some of my kindergarten students would say to me, "When I grow up, I want to be a teacher like you."

Parents and other family members are important role models for children. Teachers can also model important behaviors themselves, but they also teach about values, events, and people that a culture holds dear.

I agree with Detzner and Hiong who stated in this article that immigrant parents encourage their children to achieve high levels of education and become good citizens of their new country, and that most of the immigrant parents may have difficulty in learning a new language.

In my opinion concerning immigrant parents and children, as well as other minority groups, they are all challenged more by their past experiences and may experience problems with reconciling the traditional standards and expectations of contemporary American society.

In all public schools, these students are taught the same skills, finding created ways to illustrate the relevance of educational content to real-life experiences, and to connect students' prior knowledge, life experiences, and interests with learning goals.

It is also necessary for all teachers to plan instructional and designed learning experiences for all students, drawing on and valuing students' backgrounds, interests, and developmental learning needs. They also need to modify instructional plans to adjust for students' needs.

Lastly, teachers should use a variety of instructional strategies and resources to respond to students' diverse needs. They should also collect and use multiple sources of information to assess student learning.

Chapter 16

Teacher Portfolios

I AGREE THAT TEACHER PORTFOLIOS are an effective way to assess teacher performance and enhance learning.

I also believe that the overall goal of assessment is to collect information regarding a targeted program and its effectiveness in relation to the criteria.

I agree with both Fetterman and Shadish that through such evaluations, one can examine the appropriateness of the program and teacher's performance in early childhood education.

It is my belief that the format of teacher's portfolio should be structured and well organized. It should include purpose, goals, and program objectives, listed as follows:

1. Purpose
   - Provide strategies and activities for meeting the needs of all students.
   - Provide a wide range of assessment tools to measure student achievement before, during, and after instruction.
2. Program Goals
   - Provide high-quality curriculum and instruction so that all students can meet or exceed district academic content standards aligned with the California Standards for the

teaching profession in reading, writing, listening, speaking, and across the curriculum in grades K–12.

3. Program Objectives
- Provide students with many opportunities to develop skills through meaningful activities and strategies in all academics across the curriculum.
- Provide opportunities for all students to explore interesting and familiar topics that will help them expand their knowledge and examine new ideas that are related to the subject, based on their own research.

I agree with Steegins when he said that researchers have found that teachers spend significant amounts of time being engaged in assessment-related activities for their students, but they do not apply this standard of assessment to their own performance.

I also agree with this article because it states that there is an effective way to assess teacher performance and enhance learning, meaning that it discusses the procedures and methods of development assessment for teachers with the purpose of helping teachers evaluate their own performance as well as the effectiveness of the program.

Finally, I also agree with the article because it states the primary goal of teacher portfolios, and that is to describe, through documentation over an extended period of time, the full range of a teacher's abilities and effectiveness to use the results of assessments to improve student learning.

I think a good example of this is for teachers to ask themselves the following questions:

1. What strategies did I use in my lesson?
2. What skills did I teach in my lesson?

3. What behavioral observations did I make?
4. How might I extend my lesson?
5. Did I allow enough time for students to ask questions?
6. What questions did I ask?
- In assessing students' learning, did I do the following:
  - Collect and use multiple sources of information to assess student learning?
  - Use the results of assessments to improve my skills in communication with students, families and others?

I was influenced by the statement made in this article by Tabor. He indicated that non-English-speaking young children under the age of 6 years do not have sufficient support in an optimal learning environment for school-age children, and few studies have been conducted concerning these very young children. Therefore, research is needed on how educators create a supportive learning environment for children who have limited English proficiency in a preschool setting.

Tabor also stated that this will help educators increase their understanding of children's unique needs in a culturally and linguistically diverse classroom, which, in turn, will make these children's preschool lives more meaningful and enjoyable.

I firmly agree with Tabor's statement concerning the fact that more research is needed to help teachers create a more supportive learning environment for these students who have limited English proficiency in a preschool program.

I was a participant in a staff development program known as (SDAIE), which means Specifically Designed Academic Instruction In English.

This program was developed for LEP students (Limited English Proficiency) to help educators to reflect on their experiences and knowledge in content areas using teaching strategies to help LEP students understand the curriculum. These strategies include using nonverbal cues to convey content, such as demonstrations, pictures, graphic organizers, etc., as well as verbal supports to convey content, e.g., paraphrasing, repeating, and checking for understanding.

The SDAIE teaching and learning strategies are effective for LEP students and provide those students with maximum access to learning.

I learned that the SDAIE lessons work best with cooperative grouping activities for small groups and that all lessons should focus on the students' prior knowledge and vocabulary.

Most important of all in my understanding of the SDAIE program is that all lessons should include the four domains of language, which are listening, speaking, reading, and writing.

In my experience in applying the SDAIE lessons to LEP students' learning and activities experiences, I provided those students with activities for their personal intellectual growth, interest, and an appreciation of student achievement.

As a participant in the SDAIE program for staff development, I learned that the program is very consistent with the guidelines and content areas in and throughout the curriculum. Rubrics were developed in our district to accommodate student learning in grades K–6, and to help teachers better understand how to develop and sequence instructional activities and materials for student learning. They also drew on and displayed value of the students' background, interests, and developmental learning needs.

Rubrics were used, and were very helpful and appropriate, for scoring. An example of the rubric I used was for writing performances in kindergarten and first grade. Initial letters A, B, C, and D were used to record student points beginning with the highest score point. Examples:

Score Point 4-A Advanced

a) Student writing with the picture or prompt (kindergarteners may dictate)
b) Writes one or more sentences using proper mechanics and usage
c) Correct letter formation—no reversals
d) Proper spacing, spelling, punctuation, or language usage

Score Point 3-B Proficient

a) Writing is easily understood
b) Expresses complete thoughts, although may not use standard sentences
c) No more than four errors in mechanics, spacing, periods, or capitals

Score Point 2-C Basic

a) May write down letters/numbers to represent words
b) Can write first/last name properly
c) Demonstrates limited sounds/symbols of relationship of words
d) Demonstrates understanding of word boundaries

Score Point 1-D Below Basic

a) No symbolic representations of words and numbers
b) It is difficult to tell what this child wrote
c) Does not demonstrate sound/symbol of relationship of a word
d) Illegible writing of first/last name

Score Point 0-F No Response

I highly recommend that teachers use the SDAIE lesson plan with LEP (Limited English Proficiency) students and also in a preschool setting, using cooperative grouping and designed lessons that includes the SDAIE teaching strategies with students. Get students involved in real-life experiences that take them into, through, and beyond the text using the domains of language that are listening, speaking, reading, and writing.

I have included two teacher lesson plans I used in the classroom with my kindergarten students, one in Language Arts and the other a SDAIE lesson in math.

As a result, both lessons were very successful. These lessons required a great deal of planning, teacher modeling, and checking for understanding. I learned to look carefully at the methods and assessment that emphasize LEP students learning content area through English by providing ongoing monitoring and assessment strategies that allow students to demonstrate learning through written, oral, visual, kinesthetic, auditory, and portfolio assessment.

Chapter 17

Teaching and Learning Experiences in Early Childhood Education

by Velma Melancon

For over a decade, I served as a mentor-teacher in a multicultural and multilingual school population with the responsibility to create and manage school environments that are fair, enabling, and effective in the Lynwood Unified School District (LUSD). This involved teaching in innovative ways that encouraged learning; developing relevant curriculum; connecting students' prior knowledge, life experiences, and interests with learning goals, using a variety of instructional strategies and resources to respond to students' diverse needs.

The purpose of the mentor-teacher program was to provide intensive learning experiences for beginning teachers. Since California has provided professional teaching practices to facilitate the induction of beginning teachers into their professional roles and responsibilities, California provided a common language and a new vision of the scope and complexity of teaching. A set of California Standards for the Teaching Profession was developed to formulate professional goals to improve teaching practices.

The California Standards are organized around six interrelated categories of teaching practice.

The six standards are:

- Engaging and supporting all students in learning

- Creating and maintaining effective environments for student learning
- Understanding and organizing subject matter for student learning
- Planning instruction and designing learning experiences for all students
- Assessing student learning
- Developing as professional educators

These six standards represent a developmental, holistic view of teaching, and are intended to meet the needs of diverse teachers and students in the State of California. The set of standards provide quality and effectiveness for beginning teacher support and assessment programs. The programs have also been developed to guide the design, implementation, and operation of programs to facilitate the induction of beginning teachers.

The California Standards are introduced in a narrative description of practice that portrays an accomplished level of professional teaching. Each standard is organized in elements that identify key areas within that domain of teaching. Each element is also specified with questions that encourage teachers to explore aspects of teaching practice throughout their careers.

Purposes and Uses of the California Teaching Standards

As first-year and second-year teachers continue to develop through intensive learning activities, they build on their preservice preparation that lead to lifelong professional development. These standards are designed to be used by teachers to:

- prompt reflection about student learning and teaching practice;

- formulate professional goals to improve teaching practice;
- guide, monitor, and assess the progress of a teacher's practice toward professional goals and professionally accepted benchmarks.

Finally, the California Standards for the Teaching Profession are based on current research and expert advice pertaining to the best teaching practices. The standards address the diversity of students and teachers in California schools today, and reflect a holistic, developmental view of teaching.

Context of Teaching in California

Professional educators in the State of California are serving the most diverse population of students in the history of education. The diversity among students can greatly enrich and enliven the educational experience. There is a critical need for teachers who are responsive to the diverse cultural, racial, religious, ethnic, linguistic, and socioeconomic backgrounds of all students. The California Standards for the Teaching Profession support the creation of inclusive classrooms, in which diverse students with varying learning styles and abilities are engaged and challenged as learners. The standards reflect an expectation that the education of diverse students is likely to be most productive when teachers use effective pedagogical principles and practices in all subject areas.

This text was written to help educators develop a broad perspective in planning instruction to create and maintain an effective environment for student learning as we enter into the twenty-first century. Learning to teach in an urban setting, drawing on and valuing students' backgrounds, interests, and developmental learning needs, are vitally important. How these children learn, sequencing instructional activities and materials for student learning, connecting students' prior knowledge, life experiences, and interests with learning goals, are all part of the equation. It is also necessary to use a variety of instructional strategies and resources to respond to students' diverse needs and collect and use multiple sources of information to assess student learning.

I believe that all students learn best when the curriculum is relevant to their lives, when it is of personal interest to them, and when they are actively engaged in the pursuit of knowledge.

The curriculum must be flexible so that teachers are able to construct lessons that will be of high interest to their unique group of students, and actively engage them in creating knowledge, using a variety of instructional strategies and resources. This book address individual needs, as well as connecting students' prior knowledge, life experiences, and interests, along with facilitating learning experiences that promote autonomy, interaction, and choice.

The text also addresses the need of using the results of addressing student learning, guiding instruction, communicating with students, families, and other audiences about student progress, life experiences, and interests.

I also believe that all students should be involved in a literature and critical thinking program to engage them in a discovery process which clarifies thinking, increases knowledge, and deepens their understanding of human issues and social values.

I further believe that educators should focus on more innovated teaching methods that highlight educational objectives such as Blooms Taxonomy that extends students' thinking in the following areas:

- Recall: Learning the information
- Comprehension: Understanding the information
- Application: Using the information
- Analysis: Examining specific parts of the information
- Synthesis: Doing something new and different with the information

Evaluation: Judging the information

Researchers have found that teachers spend significant amounts of time being engaged in assessment-related activities for their students, but they do not apply this standard of assessment to their own performance. Teacher portfolios are an effective way to assess teacher performance and enhance learning.

I firmly believe that the format of a teacher's portfolio should be structured and well organized. It should include purpose, goals, and program objectives, listed as follows:

1. Purpose
   - Provide strategies and activities for meeting the needs of all students.
   - Provide a wide range of assessment tools to measure student achievement.

2. Program Goals
   - Provide high-quality curriculum and instruction so that all students will meet or exceed district academic content standards for the teaching profession in reading, writing, listening, speaking, and throughout the curriculum in grades K–8.

3. Program Objectives
   - Provide students with meaningful activities and strategies and academics throughout the curriculum.
   - Provide opportunities for all students to explore interesting and familiar topics that will help them expand their knowledge and examine new ideas that are related to the subject, based on their own research.

Therefore, the primary goal for teacher portfolios is to describe, through documentation over an extended period of time, the full range of a teacher's abilities and effectiveness to use the results of assessments to improve student learning.

Ask yourself in assessing students' learning, did I do the following:
- Collect and use multiple sources of information?

- Use the results of assessments to improve my skills in communication with students, families, and others?

In order to help educators increase their understanding of children's unique needs in a culturally and linguistically diverse classroom, which will make these children's preschool lives more meaningful and enjoyable, further research is needed to help teachers create a more supportive learning environment for these students who have limited English proficiency in a preschool program.

The Preschool Years, Ages Two to Five

Children are born with characteristic ways of behaving and reacting (temperaments). Some children are active, others are quiet; some are slow to warm up, others quite sociable. Parents, too, have styles of responding, which are results of their own inborn temperaments and their experiences. The match between the style of the parent and that of the child significantly affects how the child develops. This is to say that the parents do have a formative influence on their children within the context of their child's and their own temperaments.

The circumstances of the children's immediate world affect them, from their friends and neighbors, to the choice of preschools that exist in their communities. The larger world has an impact of too rapid technological change, the plague of AIDS, and stranger danger.

Children grow up in micro- and macroenvironments, and are affected by both these settings. Children then begin to develop images of how the world is. For example, how mothers and fathers act or what toys are appropriate for "boys" versus "girls." Such expectations guide their behavior and form the basis of their concepts. As children encounter new information and experiences, they revise their ideas and gain new understanding about how the world works and what people are like, including themselves.

Adults and parents, too, have expectations about the events they encounter. When their experiences clash with these expectations, they feel pain, guilt, anger, disappointment, and get upset. However, this is a part of the process of realigning their expectations and experiences (either by changing to live up to their images or adapting these images to be more realistic) as they grow. Therefore, progress for parents and adults can teach children how to resolve some of the problems that confront them in the normal course of growing up.

Listening to and respecting preschoolers' ideas and signals may take time, but in the long term, the listening and respect help children became independent, self-confident, curious, and creative. At best, those we rely on should enable us and enlarge our perspective, so that we emerge from these supportive relationships more able to appreciate ourselves and our children.

The writer was a participant in a staff development program known as SDAIE, which means Specially Designed Academic Instruction in English. This program was developed for LEP students (Limited English Proficiency) to help teachers reflect on their knowledge and experiences in content areas, using teaching strategies so that LEP students can understand the curriculum. These strategies included using nonverbal cues to convert content, such as demonstrations, pictures, graphic organizers, as well as verbal supports, to convey content, such as paraphrasing, repeating, and checking for understanding.

The SDAIE teaching and learning strategies are effective for LEP students and provide those students with maximum assess to learning. I learned that SDAIE lessons work best with cooperative grouping activities for small group instruction and that all lessons should focus on the students' prior knowledge and vocabulary.

Most importantly, my understanding of the SDAIE instructional program is that all lessons should include the four domains of language: listening, speaking, reading, and writing throughout the curriculum.

In my teaching and learning experiences, in applying the lesson to LEP students' learning activities and strategies, this lesson works well with all students for their personal and intellectual growth in early childhood education.

I highly recommend that first-year teachers use the SDAIE lesson plan with LEP (Limited English Proficiency) students, and also in preschool programs use cooperative grouping and designed lessons. They should include domains of language in listening and speaking strategies to help them share information, opinions, and questions as they listen to appropriate literary selections read aloud daily. This will also help students to speak in clear and coherent sentences.

I have included in this text two teacher lesson plans which were developed with my kindergarten students, using the SDAIE program, one in Language Arts which is literature-based, and the other SDAIE lesson plan in math.

As a result, both lessons were very successful. Both lessons were highly structured and required a great deal of planning and checking for understanding. I looked carefully at the methods and assessment that emphasized learning in the content area for both lessons. I provided ongoing assessment to allow students to demonstrate their learning abilities through written, oral, visual, kinesthetic, auditory, and portfolios.

The SDAIE (Specifically Designed Academic Instructions in English) program is the key for educational change and is desperately needed in preparing our students for future learning in the twenty-first century. Change is absolutely necessary for teachers to establish a climate that promotes fairness and respect. Teachers must also modify instructional plans to adjust for students' needs and use a variety of instructional strategies and resources to respond to the diversity of those needs.

Preservice training and in-service development of teachers in an age of scientific acceleration and technological advancement presents complex problems for educators that may result in unproductive teaching concepts and practices.

Beginning teachers need support and assessment programs to guide and design short-term and long-term plans, to foster student learning, and also to develop and sequence instructional activities and materials.

Educators should, and must, establish professional goals, pursue opportunities to grow in well planned instruction, implement goals and creative activities which are designed to meet the needs of all students, thus, enabling them to apply their knowledge and confidence in becoming lifelong learners and productive members of society.

Developing as a professional during this process of teaching and learning, educators should be required to work within communities to improve professional practice, work with families, and work with colleagues to further improve professional development. The obsolescence skills, knowledge, and competencies in teaching dictates the need for continuous staff development.

Recent technological advancements have sharpened the awareness of and the needs for educational innovations that contribute to effective teaching.

Most importantly of all, teachers need to:

- Love children.
- Understand their cultural background.
- Be involved in a multicultural, multiethnic training program.
- Involve parents working together with schools and communities as a team of collaborators to motivate students.
- Strive for excellence and serve as a role model.
- Get to know leaders in the communities.
- Plan field trips within the community that will help students appreciate where they live.
- Invite community leaders to be a part of the school program.

Teachers should create physical environments that engage all students in learning to promote social development, as well as maintaining higher standards for student behavior, which also supports students' learning.

Chapter 18

The Challenge for Early Childhood Education in the Twenty-First Century

WE ARE NOW FACING A CHALLENGE in education in the twenty-first century in America. The nature of teaching requires continuous growth in order to engage and challenge increasingly diverse students in a rapidly changing world. Teachers are never finished as professional leaders, no matter how extensive or excellent their formal education and preparation. If teachers' expertise, capabilities, and accomplishments are to be enriched over time, the teachers must become reflective practitioners who actively seek to strengthen and augment their professional skills, knowledge, and perspectives throughout their careers.

The challenge remains unchanged if veteran and experienced teachers are not an integral part of the state's efforts to support new teachers entering the profession in different areas of teaching as students develop in different curriculum areas as individuals. Beginning teachers can develop their skills and move forward in their professional practice. With the help and support of experienced teachers' mentoring, monitoring, and assessing areas, that are essential to new teachers' development and success in following standards that describe best teaching practices at an accomplished level, beginning teachers will find the standards useful to guide their developing practice for professional growth, with an experienced support teacher to facilitate.

The California Standards for the Teaching Profession reflect a developmental view of teaching and are an integral part of the state's efforts to foster excellence in teaching and learning.

The California Standards for the Teaching Profession is a developmental view of teaching, and gives particular attention to the early years of teacher performance regarding instructional strategies and new ways to support students' learning, building on students' prior knowledge, life experiences, and interests. These standards help to achieve learning goals for all students engaged in a variety of skills and activities that are challenging learning experiences for their diverse needs. Teachers must facilitate challenging learning experiences for students in environments that promote autonomy, interaction, and choice.

With globalization, increased mobility of families, and the resultant changes to the social and cultural profiles of other countries, early childhood education can be exciting and challenging for teachers.

For many years, teachers have tried to respond to the diverse needs of individual children. They have been concerned with planning and implementing developmentally appropriate curriculum.

The focus now is to examine the complexities of the contemporary contexts of teaching what we know now and explore what we know about the challenges of responding to social cultural diversity, as will as develop a framework. Early Literacy Learning will include elements and values for creating instructional approaches in a balanced literacy program.

Bringing Early Literacy to Life

Since literacy is the ability to read and write, young children appear to learn about written language before school, which is within their cultures. As they participate in literacy events, utilizing these forms of written language, they learn that print is a language signifier, and that it carries meaning, and they learn about the ways in which print represents meaning.

I completed the course "Training in California Early Literacy Learning" in the LUSD (Lynwood Unified School District). I planned and developed lessons with my kindergarten students in reading and writing activities. Along with the designed lessons and instructional strategies, various elements were used to motivate children to read, develop a sense of the story, and develop an ability to write words and use punctuation.

After completing the course in Early Literacy Learning, I was able to plan and develop activities that included eight elements and their values to guide instructions. Two important elements that I thought most important were used in the instructional planning. They are as follows.

1. Shared Writing

   Writing with children to:
   - Learn conventions of punctuation, grammar, and concepts about print.
   - Learn the writing process.
   - Learn spelling in context, and develop style and voice.

2. Independent Writing

   Writing by children to:
   - Practice learned conventions.
   - Develop understanding of audiences.
   - Support reading development.
   - Practice spelling strategies and,
   - Develop authentic writing purposes.

Interactive writing was used for skills development. Interactive writing is teacher-supported and student writing. It demonstrates the concept of print, early strategies, and how words work. It also provides opportunities to hear sounds in words and connect with letters, as well as helps children understand processes in reading and writing. It also provides opportunities to plan and construct texts. A variety of instructional strategies and resources were used in response to students' needs. Reading aloud to children, reading new stories, and rereading favorite selections motivates children to read, provides an adult demonstration, develops a sense of story, and increases a child's vocabulary.

One of the most favorite stories in my kindergarten class was *Caps for Sale* by Esphyr Slobodkina, a core literature book for this grade level.

This selection is highly recommended in literature for all kindergarten students, and is very appropriate for early literacy learning.

Readers may refer to the SDAIE Lesson Plan, Chapter 9, Rubric 3, page 95 for further instructions, the theme of *Caps for Sale*, and the instructional goals for bringing early literacy to life focused on linking content areas and concepts utilizing students' skills and abilities to learn the writing process to read with meaning, learn spelling in context, and the ability to use punctuation.

In planning this selection, I used the 5 Steps Lesson Plan. The elements of this lesson plan are as follows:

1. Anticipatory Set
   Elements of Instruction:
   - 1. Focus
   - 2. Objective
   - 3. Purpose
   - 4. Transfer of previous learning

2. Instruction

   Elements of Instruction:
   - 1. Pretest
   - 2. Peel-off
   - 3. Provide information
   - 4. Model
   - 5. Check for understanding

3. Divided Practice

   Elements of Divided Practice:
   - 1. Mass practice with teacher
   - 2. Student response demonstrating learning
   - 3. Specific feedback

4. Closure

   Elements of Closure:
   - 1. Student state the learning
   - 2. Student demonstrates the learning

5. Independent Practice

   Elements of Independent Practice:
   - 1. Practice without a teacher
   - 2. Careful monitoring
   - 3. Immediate feedback

Students were given a Venn diagram worksheet and were asked to choose their favorite story, use the Venn diagram to compare and contrast it with the story, *Caps for Sell*; they were instructed to draw pictures to show what was alike, what was different, and what was the same about both stories.

This instructional activity was used to increase each student's active participation in learning. Opportunities were provided for all students to share, discuss, interact, and build on their prior knowledge and interests to make the content relevant and meaningful to them.

Finally, the success of the training in the California Early Literacy Learning Program was to provide leadership as a Literacy Coordinator, i.e., share experiences with staff and develop programs to enhance student learning. Also, the literacy coordinator is to fully participate in the implementation of the program in their local sites.

The focus of the leadership training program concentrated on leadership development, peer coaching techniques, and construction of staff development modules that can then be used in subsequent years. The leadership training also provided training for first-year teachers to demonstrate and refine their staff development training techniques that build on their preservice preparation and lead to lifelong professional development.

Velma Melancon

As a twenty-eight-year experienced teacher with the Lynwood Unified School District elementary education grades K–6, as well as an associate professor at Los Angeles Southwest College for over a decade, and an instructor, teaching child development courses at Drew University, I have successfully experienced the following:

Presenter/Trainer
- Certified trainer for "teaching strategies for young children drug-exposed and at risk."
- UCLA Instructional Leaders Participant
- UCLA Language Arts Instructional Leadership Participant
- UCLA Mathematics Instructional Leadership Participant
- SDAIE

Specifically Designed Academic Instruction in English Participant Certificate of Completion
- Participant in the Peer Assistance and Review Consulting Teaching Training
- Developed Social Studies Competencies Grade 2 Presenter
- Program Quality Review Participant
- Direct Instruction Beginning Teachers Monitor and Assist (school site)
- SESAT 2 Kindergarten Developed Practice Test in Reading
- LUSD (Lynwood Unified School District) Language Arts Academic Content Standards Grades K–8 Curriculum Committee
- Second Annual Symposium Los Angeles Airport Marriott Hotel "Teaching Strategies for Young Children Drug Exposed and At-risk" Presenter

- "Teaching Strategies for Young Children Drug-Exposed and At-Risk" LUSD Elementary Principals Presenter
- Los Angeles Southwest College Second Annual Early Childhood Conference "Our Children's Education Our Link to the Future" Participant
- Los Angeles Southwest College Professional Development Activities: "Teaching Strategies for Young Children Drug-Exposed and At-Risk" Presenter

This presentation was designed for staff who have previously attended the Hillsborough training course, as well as others. Trainers were asked to share experiences with groups, teachers, educators, and new materials, including adaptations for parent training which was also available to certificated trainers. Strategies to involve administrators were discussed at the Los Angeles County Office of Education 2nd Annual Symposium.

Glossary

accommodation. Piaget's term for the kind of adaptation that involves modifying a previously used action or idea to suit a new situation.

adaptation. In Piaget's view, the process of change that results from having to deal with, and adjust to, the environment.

adolescents into adults. Development includes changes in size and shape, in reasoning ability and knowledge, in motor ability, in the ability to communicate.

aggression. Physical or verbal acts directed against people, animals, or things, and performed with the intention of hurting, damaging, or destroying.

assimilation. Piaget's term for the kind of adaptation that involves applying an already known action or idea to a new object or situation.

associative play. A type of interactive play that involves two or more children doing the same thing and doing it together, but with no attempt to organize the activity or to take turns.

attachment. The bond of affection and dependency felt by a child for another person, which makes the child want to be near that other person and turn to him or her for comfort in times of stress.

autonomy. Self-determination, independence. The ability to decide for oneself what one is going to do.

autonomy versus shame and doubt. In Erikson's view, this stage occurs between 2 and 3 years old, and it is the second stage of development. Toddlers are assumed to be engaged in a struggle for self-determination, while at the same time, doubting their capabilities to achieve and to be "good."

basic trust versus mistrust. In Erikson's theory, this first stage of development occurs during infancy. Babies are assumed to develop basic trust if they come to feel that their parents can be relied upon.

behavior modification. The use of the principles of operant conditioning to change the behavior of an organism.

behaviorism. The school of psychology that concerns itself with observable behavior, rather than "inner" things such as thoughts and feelings. Behaviorists stress the importance of the environment (rather than of hereditary factors) and study how organisms learn as a result of their experiences.

case study. A descriptive study that involves, in most cases, only a single subject—often one who is unusual in some way.

classical conditioning. The conditioning of a simple automatic, inborn response to a neutral stimulus by pairing the neutral stimulus with a stimulus that already evokes the response. Eventually, the neutral stimulus alone is able to evoke the response.

cognitive behaviorism. A branch of social learning theory which posits that reinforcements and punishments may be effective even if they're not experienced directly, but are only observed being given to another person (a model). These observed reinforcements and punishments are assumed to influence the observer's later behavior through a learning process that is cognitive.

cognitive development. The development of the capacity to think, to reason, and to understand.

cognitive-developmental theory. Piaget's theory of cognitive development.

concrete operations, period of. In Piagetian theory, the period of development beginning around age 7 and ending around age 11. Children in this period can consider several aspects of a situation at once, but their understanding is tied to real (concrete) objects and events.

developmental psychology. The branch of psychology that studies the processes of growth and maturation and the effects of experience.

disadvantaged. Families or homes are referred to as disadvantaged when they are headed by individuals who are employed in unskilled, low-paying jobs or are unemployed, and who have relatively little education.

ego. According to Freud, one of the three aspects of the human mind. The ego is the thinking, rationale part.

egocentric thought. In Piaget's view, the way preoperational children think, characterized by an inability to see things from someone else's point of view.

elaboration. A technique used to help in remembering something. Verbal ideas or visual images are thought up as memory aids as a way of connecting two stimuli in paired associate learning.

empathy. The tendency to feel sad when another person is hurt or distressed, and to feel pleased when another person is happy. The ability to share in other people's feelings.

environment. Any aspects of the world that a child experiences in any way, or that can affect the child in any way, are part of the child's environment.

experimental method. A method for carrying out research that involves doing something—for example, treating a group of subjects in a particular way—and observing the results. Typically, that group of subjects is compared to a control group, who did not receive that treatment.

formal operations, period of. In Piagetian theory, the period of development that begins around age 11. It is characterized by the ability to reason abstractly and to test possible solutions to a problem in a symptomatic way.

formal teaching. A traditional style: children are told where to sit and what to do; homework and tests are given and graded.

foster child. A child who is living temporarily in a foster home, either because a permanent adoptive home has not yet been found, or because his or her biological parents have not released the child for adoption.

foster parent. A person taking care of a foster child in his or her home. Foster parents usually receive a small salary to cover the expenses of caring for foster children.

generalize. To transfer a learned response or concept to another stimulus or situation similar (but not identical) to the one involved in the original learning.

heredity. A term used to refer to inherited or genetic characteristics—characteristics carried by the genes.

id. According to Freud, one of the three aspects the human mind. The id is present from birth and is the home of powerful instinctive desires such as hunger, thirst, and the sexual urge.

identity. A principle used in solving a Piagetian conservation problem. If the problem involves, for example, liquid volume, the identity principle would be the idea that a certain amount of water remains the same amount regardless of the height or width of the glass.

impulsive. Kagan's term for children who respond quickly on the Matching Familiar Figures Test and who make a lot of errors. Such children tend to do less well in school than reflective children; they tend to jump to conclusions and to take risks.

industry versus inferiority. In Erikson's theory, the central issue during middle childhood. The conflict is between children's desire to learn the skills they will need as adults and the fear of failure.

infancy. The period of development that starts at birth and ends when the infant becomes a toddler and begins to use walking as the chief means of getting from one place to another.

informal teaching. A teaching style in which children are permitted a good deal of freedom to sit (or stand) where they wish; generally, grades are not given. Also known as the "open classroom."

initiative versus guilt. In Erikson's view, the central issue during the preschool period. Initiative arises as a result of the child's emerging ability to work toward a goal; guilt arises as a consequence of the development of the superego.

insecure attachment. A description of the quality of a child's relationship with another person, generally, a parent. A child who is insecurely attached to his mother, for example, will not greet her with happiness after being separated from her. He may ignore her, act angry at her, or alternate between two conflicting kinds or behaviors.

instinct. An inborn pattern of behavior, nowadays more often called specific behavior.

interaction. An interaction between two people occurs when each person performs some action for a series of actions in regard to the other person. The actions can include speaking to the other person, kissing, hitting, or smiling at the other person, and so on.

internalize. To take on someone else's values or standards of behavior as one's own; to believe in them.

IQ. An abbreviation of intelligence quotient. Nowadays, however, a child's IQ is not calculated by dividing mental age by chronological age, but by comparing the child's performance on an IQ test with that of other children of the same age. The IQ score is presumed to be an indication of intellectual ability.

long-term memory. "Permanent" memory, capable of retaining information for an indefinite length of time; information stored in long-term memory must first have been in short-term memory, but not all the information in short-term memory enters long-term memory.

longitudinal study. A method of studying developmental changes by observing or testing a group of subjects repeatedly over a period of time.

maturation. Development—after physical or motor development—of a sort that is assumed to result from genetic preprogramming or the gradual carrying out of a plan determined by the genes.

mental age. How advanced a child is in his or her intellectual abilities and knowledge. For instance, an intellectually average 6-year-old would have the mental age of a 6-year-old child; a gifted one might have the mental age of a child 7 or 8.

model. A person (e.g., an adult) who does something that another person (e.g., a child) might imitate.

modeling. Bandura's term for what a model does. An action performed by a model, possibly with the idea that an observer (e.g., a child) may initiate that action.

motor development. The development of the ability to move and coordinate the parts of the body, as in crawling, walking, grasping things with the hands, and so on.

motor pattern. The basic sequence of movements involved in performing some action, for example, walking or running.

motor skill. The ability to perform a motor pattern with some degree of smoothness and precision.

neonate. A newborn human baby.

nuclear family. A family consisting of a husband, a wife, and their children.

nurture. A term used to refer to the way a child is reared or (when contrasted with nature) to refer to environment in general.

object permanence. In Piagetian theory, the concept that things have permanent existence in the world, even if they can't be seen at the moment.

observational learning. Learning that is acquired through watching other people's behavior and through seeing the consequences that result from their behavior.

open classroom. A classroom in which teaching is informal—children are allowed to select their own activities and to sit (or stand) wherever they wish. In many cases, walls between adjoining classrooms are removed so that the children in a single open classroom may be from two or more grades.

operant conditioning. Skinner's term for the process that occurs when an organism is reinforced for making a particular response. When a response is reinforced, it is more likely to be made again.

parallel play. When two (or more) children play side by side at the same activity, paying little or no attention to each other.

peer group. The group of children of roughly the same age with whom a child interacts at school or elsewhere and who are presumed to share common values, standards of behavior, and so on.

peers. A child's peers are other children of roughly the same age with whom he or she interacts in some way.

person permanence. The concept that people continue to exist even when they can't be seen or heard.

phonics. The correspondences between the sounds of spoken words and the letters of written words that exist in English (and in other languages) written in alphabetic symbols. Children who are taught phonics when they're learning to read are taught to "sound out" written words.

prenatal. before birth.

prenatal period. The period that begins at conception and ends at birth.

preoperational period. In Piagetian theory, the second major period of development—roughly from age 2 to age 7. The preoperational child, according to Piaget, can use mental representations but cannot adopt another person's point of view and cannot decenter.

preschool period. The period of development that begins around the age 2½ and ends when the child enters first grade, usually around age 6.

prosocial. A term used to describe behaviors that benefit others, e.g., sharing, cooperating, and helping.

psychiatrist. A person who has been through medical school, obtained an M.D. degree, and then gone on to study human personality, with a particular emphasis on psychological problems. Most psychiatrists see patients and administer psychotherapy or drug treatment.

psychoanalysis. A method of psychotherapy devised by Freud and based on his theories that is still in use today.

psychoanalytic theory. A theory of human personality and development originated by Sigmund Freud which stresses the importance of unconscious motivations, particularly those of a sexual nature.

psychologist. A person who studies human (or, in some cases, animal) behavior, or personality, or cognition, or learning, or memory, or sensation and perception, either from a scientific or a clinical viewpoint. Some administer psychotherapy. Most psychologists have a Ph.D. degree from the graduate division of a university psychology department.

psychosocial. A term used to describe Erikson's theory (as opposed to Freud's, which is called psychosexual). Erikson puts more emphasis on social interactions, less on sexual matters.

punishment. The administration of something unpleasant, such as a stimulus that causes pain or the removal or something pleasant, such as food.

recognition. When contrasted with recall, a memory test that involves only a decision about whether a given stimulus is or isn't the correct one, or whether it has or hasn't been seen (or heard) before.

reflective. Kagan's term for children who respond slowly on the Matching Familiar Figures Test and who make few errors. Such children tend to do better in their schoolwork than impulsive children; they tend to be careful and analytical.

reinforcement. The administration of a reinforcer.

reliability. A test is said to have reliability when a child who takes it on Monday makes roughly the same score that she would have made if she had taken it on Friday. A reliable test, in other words, is one that is not very much affected by chance factors or day-to-day variations.

representational thought. Mental processes that make use of representations.

representations. Mental images of things previously seen, heard, or otherwise experienced; arbitrary symbols (such as words) used for thoughts about actions or things.

response. An action—often, an action that occurs after exposure to a stimulus.

reversibility. A principle used in solving a Piagetian conservation problem. If the problem involves, for example, liquid volume, the reversibility principle would be the idea that we could pour the water back into the original container and it would look the same as it did at first.

role model. An older person performing a given social or family role, whose behavior can serve as a model for a younger person to follow.

scheme. In Piagetian theory, a simple or complex pattern of action or thought that functions as a unit.

secure attachment. A description of the quality of a child's relationship with another person, generally a parent. A child who is securely attached to his mother, for example, will greet her joyfully after having been separated from her in the "strange situation."

sensorimotor period. In Piagetian theory, roughly the first 2 years of life. By the end of this period, the child has acquired object permanence and can use mental representations.

sensorimotor play. Piaget's term for the earliest type of play which involves moving the body and usually doing something to an object or objects. Shaking a rattle and building a tower with blocks are examples.

short-term memory. Temporary memory, capable of holding a small number of items (such as numbers) for a short period of time or for as long as they are retained by means of rehearsal.

sibling. A brother or a sister.

social learning theory. The view that children learn through observing others, as well as through the reinforcements and punishments that they themselves receive.

social punishment. An unpleasant reaction by one person to the behavior of another—for example, frowning, criticizing, hitting, ignoring, or taking something away from the other person.

social reinforcement. A pleasant reaction by one person to the behavior of another—for example, smiling, giving praise, showing affection, complying with a request, or simply paying attention to the other person.

socialization. The aspect of development that involves the child's learning to behave according to the rules of his or her society and acquiring the attitudes, skills, and knowledge needed to get along in that society.

society. A group of people with a common culture.

solitary play. Play that involves no interaction at all with other people.

stage. A period of development that is assumed to be qualitatively different from the previous or subsequent period. Stages are also assumed to occur in a particular order, though their timing can vary.

stimulus. Anything that can be seen or heard or perceived through one of the other senses. This term is often applied to something (e.g., a picture, a sound) used in an experiment, particularly something that is expected to evoke a response.

strategy. A technique for doing something, especially one that is directed toward a particular goal. For instance, rehearsal is a metacognitive strategy for retaining words or numbers in short-term memory.

superego. According to Freud, one of the three aspects of the human mind. The superego is the equivalent of a conscience; it develops between the ages of 3 and 5½.

temperament. The persistent aspects of a person's personality—for example, how adaptable, cheerful, active, and emotional that person is.

toddlerhood. The period of development that starts when the child begins to use walking as his or her chief means of getting from one place to another and that ends around the age of 2½.

traumatic. A term applied to experiences that might have upsetting or even injurious effects.

vocalize. To say a word or to make a speechlike sound. A baby's coos and babbles are considered vocalizations.

whole-word method. A method for teaching children to read that does not involve the teaching of phonics. Children are taught to recognize words as wholes by their overall shape, instead of sounding them out letter by letter.

REFERENCES

Aries, P. *Centuries of Childhood.* New York: Knopf, 1962. 5.

Kessen, William. *The Child.* New York: Wiley, 1965. 8.

___ed. *Child in China.* London: Yale University Press, 1975. 510.

Marvick, Elizabeth W. Childhood history and decisions of state: the case of Louis XIII. History of Childhood Quarterly: T*he Journal of Psychohistory,* 1974, 2 (2), 135–80.

Piaget, J., and B. Inhelder. *The Child's Conception of Space.* London: Routledge and Kegan Paul, 1956. 179.

FURTHER READINGS

Anderson, Barry F. *The Psychology Experiment.* 2nd ed. Belmont, Calif.: Brooks/Cale, 1971. A helpful book for understanding the scientific method and how to conduct an experiment. Paperback.

Bandura, A. Influence of models' reinforcement contingencies on the acquisition of imitative responses. *Journal of Personality and Social Psychology*, 1965a, 1, 589–95; 271. Behavioral modification through modeling procedures, in L. Krasner and L.P. Ullman (eds.), Research in behavior modification. New York: Holt, Rinehart and Winston, 1965a. 280.

___A social learning interpretation of psychological dysfunctions. In P. London and D. Rosenhan (eds.). *Foundations of Abnormal Psychology*. New York: Holt, Rinehart and Winston, 1968. 514.

___*Social Learning Theory.* Morristown, N.J.: General Learning Press, 1771. 272.

Bandura, A., and F.L. Menlove. Factors determining vicarious extinction of avoidance behavior through symbolic modeling. *Journal of Personality and Social Psychology*, 1968, 8, 99–108, 494.

Bandura, A., and W. Mischel. Modification of self-imposed delay of reward through exposure to live and symbolic models. *Journal of Personality and Social Psychology,* 1965, 698–705.

Bandura, A.; Dorothea Ross, and Shelia A. Ross. Transmission of aggression imitation of aggressive models. *Journal of Abnormal and Social Psychology*, 1966a, 3–11, 13, 271.

___Vicarious reinforcement and initiative learning. *Journal of Abnormal and Social Psychology,* 1963b, 271, 601–607.

Blalock, Hubert M., Jr. *Social Research.* Englewood Cliffs, N.J.: Prentice-Hall, 1970. Explains the nature of some of the basic issues encountered in research in the social sciences. Paperback.

De Mause, Lloyd (ed.). *The History of Childhood.* New York: Psychohistory Press, 1974. A survey of historical views of childhood over the last two thousand years.

Erikson, E.H. (1959). Identify and the life cycle. New York: International Universities Press.

Erikson, E.H. (1963). Childhood and Society (2nd ed.). New York: Norton.

Freud, A., and S. Dann. (1967). An experiment in group upbringing. In Y. Brackbill and G.G. Thompson (eds.). *Behavior in Infancy and Early Childhood.* New York: The Free Press.

Freud, S. (1938). The history of the psychoanalytic movement. In A.A. Brill (ed. and trans.). The basic writings of Sigmund Freud. New York: Modern Library.

___(1950). The analysis of a phobia in a five-year old boy. In Collected Papers (Vol. 1). London: Hogarth. (Originally published in 1909.)

___(1965). *New Introductory Lectures in Psychoanalysis* (J. Stackey, ed. and trans.). New York: Norton. (Originally published in 1933.)

Gesell, A. The ontogenesis of infant behavior. In L. Carmichael (ed.), *Manual of Child Psychology*, 2nd ed., pp. 355–73. New York: Wiley, 1954. 128.

Gesell, A., H.M. Halverson, H. Thompson, F.L. Ilg, B.M. Gastner, L.B. Ames, and C.S. Amatruda. *The First Five Years of Life: A Guide to the Study of the Preschool Child.* New York: Harper and Row. 1949, 131.

Gesell, A., F.L. Ilg, and L.B. Ames. *Youth: The Years from Ten to Sixteen.* New York: Harper and Row, 1956. 142.

Gesell, A., and Helen Thompson. Learning and maturation in identical twins: an experimental analysis by the method of co-twin control. Genetic Psychology Monographs, 1929, 6-5-124, 123, 125, 138.

Hall, G.S. *Adolescence.* New York: Appleton, 1904. 11.

Locke, John L. Phonetic medication in four-year-old children. *Psychonomic Science,* 1971, 23 (6): 235, 409.

Locke, John L., and Virginia L. Locke. Recall of phonetically and semantically similar words by 3-year-old children. P*sychonomic Science,* 1971. 24 (4):189–90, 235

Martin, J.A., B.E. Hamilton, S.J. Ventura, F. Menacker, and M.M. Park. (2002). Births: Final data for 2000. National Vital Statistics Reports, 50 (5). Hyattsville, Maryland: National Center of Health Statistics. 20.

Maslow, Abraham. *Motivation and Personality*, 2nd ed. New York: Harper and Row, 1970. 443–44.

Medinnus, Gene R. *Child Study and Observation Guide.* New York: Wiley, 1976. A guide to observing children under different conditions and using different observational techniques. Also includes a series of observation projects. Paperback.

Piaget, J. The language and thought of the child. London: Routledge and Kegan Paul, 1926. 162–89.

___The child's conception of physical causality. London: Routledge and Kegan Paul, 1930. 162–89. The moral judgment of the child. London: Routledge and Kegan Paul. 1932. 395.

___*Play Dreams and Imitation in Childhood*. New York: W.W. Norton, 1951. 162–89.

___*Origins of Intelligence in Children*. New York: W.W. Norton, 1963. 172.

___*Six Psychological Studies*. Edited by D. Elkind. New York: Random House, Vintage Books. 1968 162–89.

Piaget, J., and B. Inhelder. *The Psychology of the Child*. New York: Basic Books, 1969. 174.

Piaget, J., and Alina Szeminska. *Child's Conception of Number*. New York: Humanities Press, 1952. 162, 189.

Proctor, B.D., and J. Dalaker. (2003). Poverty in the United States: 2002. Current Population Reports, P60-222. Washington, D.C.: U.S. Bureau of the Census, 208 Washington, D.C.: U.S. Bureau of the Census 210.

Quanty, Carol, and Anthony Davis. *Observing Children*. Sherman Oaks, Calif.: Alfred, 1974. Guidelines for observing preschool children under different conditions. Paperback.

Rogers, Carl R. *Counseling and Psychotherapy*. Boston: Houghton Mifflin 1942. 357.

___*Client-centered Therapy*. Boston: Houghton Mifflin, 1951. 357.

___*On Becoming a Person*. Boston: Houghton Mifflin. 1961. 357.

Vygotsky, L.S. *Thought and Language*. Cambridge, Mass.: M.I.T. Press. 1962. 232.

Wright, Herbert F. *Recording and Analyzing Child Behavior*. New York: Harper and Row, 1967. An example for studying children in naturally occurring situations rather than under experimental conditions. Paperback.

INDEX

A

Accommodation, 39, 41, 65, 66, 197
Achievement test, 26, 27, 28
Adaptation, 38, 39, 65, 196, 197
Analysis, 33, 69, 133, 136, 170, 182
Application, 33, 53, 100, 104, 112, 124, 170, 182
Assimilation, 38, 39, 41, 65, 66, 197

B

Behavior modification, 53, 57, 58, 198, 211
 Definition, 198
 In classroom, 57
 Research evidence, 57
 Baseline observations, 58
 Rewards, 58
 Report cards, 58
Better schools, 149-150
Bloom's taxonomy, 29, 31, 170
Building blocks, 30, 170

C

Case Study, 198
 Definition, 198
Child Development,
 Twentieth Century, 19, 22, 45
Classifying teaching methods, 41
Classroom, 24-25, 42, 46, 57-58, 80-86, 98-100, 111, 144, 154, 159, 161, 165-167, 175, 178, 181, 201
Cognitive theories, 37, 53-55
Comenius, John, 21
Contemporary families, 145

D

Darwin, Charles, 22
Developmental psychologists, 45
 Disciplinary techniques, 139
 Diverse backgrounds, 79

E

Early childhood, 163, 167-168, 179, 184, 189-190, 196, 212
  Classroom, 163
  Education, 163-172
  Literacy, 166-168, 190-192, 194
Educational Psychology, 24-26, 28, 53
  Definition, 24
  Role and scope, 24
  Testing and evaluation, 26
Egocentrism, 63-64, 66-67, 76
English, Second language, 159
Equilibrium, 38
Erikson's theory, 17, 23, 51-52, 62, 198, 201, 206, 212
Ethnic diversity, 145
Evaluation, 35, 94, 135, 137, 139-141, 171, 173

F

Freud, Sigmund, 23, 62, 89
Froebel, Friedrick, 21

G

Gesell, Arnold, 24
Goals, 27
  Ideas and research, 23

H

Heredity and environment, 93
Human learning, 53
Humanistic theories, 53, 55, 61
  Maslow and Rogers, 61

I

Ideas and research, 23
Identity crisis, 52
  Erikson's theory, 52
Important changes, 47
  Preschool years 47, 74, 90-93, 183
  Character, 32-35, 47, 127
Intelligence, 28, 39, 94, 138, 202, 214
IQ scores, 94
IQ tests, 94

J

Journals, 12, 100, 102-105, 112, 123, 126
Child development, 11-12, 15-19, 23-24, 45, 62, 80, 165, 195
  Developmental psychology, 12, 23-24, 29, 53, 199

K

Kagan, Jerome, 35, 62,72, 201, 206

Knowledge, 16, 19, 21, 25, 27-28, 30-31, 36-37, 39, 42, 46, 52, 54-55, 59-60, 65, 82-86, 96, 98, 100, 103, 109, 113, 122, 142, 145, 147-148, 156-157, 160-161, 166-167, 169-172, 174-176, 179, 181-182, 184, 186, 189-190, 194, 197, 203, 208

L

Leading theorists, 23
  Erikson, Erik, 17, 23, 51-52, 62, 198, 201, 206, 212
  Freud, Sigmund, 23, 62, 89
  Hall, Stanley, 11, 23
  Maslow, Abraham, 23, 61-62, 90, 213

Piaget, Jean, 17-19, 23, 36-37, 39-41, 45-46, 49, 51-53, 59-60, 62-67, 133-138, 140, 197, 199, 200-201, 204-205, 207, 210, 214

Rogers, Carl, 23, 61-62, 90

Learning English, 161

Limitations, 41, 74

Preschool years, 47, 74, 90-93,183

Literacy, 83, 157, 167-168, 190

Literature, 29-31, 79, 82, 108, 110, 171, 182, 185

Locke, John, 15, 21, 24

M

Melancon, Velma, 195
  Lesson plan samples, 95-132
  Rubric, 95, 100, 105, 110, 112, 176, 192
  Teaching and learning, 109, 165, 176, 179, 184, 186, 190

N

Nature, 7, 12, 15, 16, 21-22, 25, 26, 53, 89, 107, 133, 139, 141, 151, 189, 203, 205, 212

Human learning, 53

O

Object permanence, 69-72, 204, 207

Organizing schemes, 65

P

Parent's Role, 56

Person permanence, 72
Pestalozzi, Johann, 22
Piaget, Jean, 17-19, 23, 36-37, 39-41, 45-46, 49, 51-53, 59-60, 62-67, 133-138, 140, 197, 199, 200-201, 204-205, 207, 210, 214
Practices and Principles, 161
Professional development, 95, 99, 106, 111, 154, 165, 180, 186, 194, 196
Psychological assessment, 87,
  Definition, 87
Psychological development, 56, 84, 90, 92
Psychological research, 87
  Case history, 88
  Experimentation, 87, 88
  Standardized test, 88
  Survey, 88
Psychology today, 89

Q

Questions, 104, 111, 113, 116, 126, 174-175, 180
  Teacher portfolios, 173

R

Rationale, 24, 147
  Educational change, 147-148, 185
  Objectives, 26-27, 29, 42, 84-85, 99, 101, 111, 116, 148, 169-170, 173-174, 182
  Student performance, 26, 82
  Psychological assessment, 87
Rousseau, J., 15, 21
  Eighteenth-century 21-22

S

Schemes, 64-65, 67, 69, 73
  Definition, 73
SDAIE, 95-96, 98-99, 107, 109-
  Definition, 107
Sherman, James, 58
Skinner, B.F., 24
Stages, 60, 62, 66-67, 69, 133
  Circular, 69-72
  Coordination, 27, 71
  Tertiary, 72
Students, 16, 19, 21, 25, 27-28, 30-31, 36-37, 39, 42, 46, 52, 54-55, 59-60, 65, 82-86, 96, 98, 100, 103, 109, 113, 122, 142, 145, 147-148
  Diverse backgrounds, 79

T

Teacher preparation, 154, 165
 Urban settings, 155-157, 165
Teaching methods, 25-26, 41-42, 163, 170, 182
 Psychological view, 42
 Testing and evaluation, 27
Theories, 15, 17, 19, 21-28, 37, 45, 51-56, 61-62, 75, 80, 84-85, 87, 133
 Influential thinkers, 15
Toddlers, 56, 91
 Frequent communication, 57
 Psychological skills, 56
 Encouragement, 94, 167
 Toward better schools, 149
 Dewey, Erikson, Montessori, Piaget, and vygotsky, 51
Twenty-first century, 13, 53, 147-148, 151-152, 181, 189
Teaching standards, 180

U

Urban settings, 155-157, 165

V

Ventimiglia, Lauren, 163, 168-171
Vygotsky, 49, 51-52, 84, 159

W

Water level, 63-64, 74
 Experiments, 74, 76

Y

Yellowbird, John, 171
 Culture of teaching, 163-169, 171

Velma Melancon: A teacher who made a difference in the lives of students is acknowledged for excellence as a Distinguished Educator in the "Who's Who Among America's Teachers; Second Edition 1992

APPENDIX

OBSERVATIONAL TOOLS

Fr. _____

Teacher　　　　Date　　　　Grade　　　　Room#

				Math			
Student Names	L/S	Reading	Writing	C	PS	S.S.	Sci
1.							
2.							
3.							
4.							
5.							
6.							
7.							
8.							
9.							
10.							
11.							
12,							
13.							
14.							
15.							
16.							
17.							
18.							
19.							

Re: Monthly Grade Level Assessment Results Subject Area Grade(s)

Kindergarten Assessment for _____

Teacher's Name:

1. Listening and Speaking

2. Reading

3. Writing

4. Math

5. Social Studies

6. Science

OBSERVATION TOOLS

Child Skills Checklist

Name: _____   Observer: _____

Program: _____   Date: _____

Directions:
- Put a *X* for items you see child perform regularly.
- Put *N* for items where there is no opportunity to observe.
- Put + for items where the child has progressed to an advanced level.
- Leave all other items blank.

1. Self-Identity

____ Separates from parents without difficulty
____ Does not cling to adults excessively
____ Makes eye contact with adults
____ Makes activity choices without teacher's help
____ Seeks other children to play with
____ Plays roles confidently in dramatic play
____ Stands up for own rights
____ Displays enthusiasm in regard to doing things for self

2. Emotional Development

____ Allows self to be comforted during stressful times
____ Eats, sleeps, toilets without fuss away from home
____ Handles sudden changes/startling situations with control
____ Can express anger in words rather than actions
____ Allows aggressive behavior to be redirected
____ Does not withdraw from others excessively

___ Shows interest/attention in classroom activities
___ Smiles, seems happy much of the time

3. Social Play

___ Plays by self with or without objects
___ Plays by self constructing or creating something
___ Plays by self in pretending-type activity
___ Plays parallel to others with or without objects
___ Plays parallel to others constructing or creating something
___ Plays parallel to others in pretending-type activity
___ Plays with a group with or without objects
___ Plays with a group constructing or creating something
___ Plays with a group in pretending-type activity

4. Prosocial Behavior

___ Shows concern for someone in distress
___ Shares something with another
___ Shows delight for someone experiencing pleasure
___ Gives something of his/her own to another
___ Takes turns with toys or activities
___ Waits for turn without a fuss
___ Helps another do task
___ Helps another in need

5. Large Motor Development

___ Walks down steps alternating feet
___ Runs with control over speed and direction
___ Jumps over obstacle landing on two feet
___ Hops forward on one foot
___ Pedals and steers tricycle

___ Climbs up and down climbing equipment with ease
___ Throws object overhand to target
___ Catches thrown object with hands

6. Small Motor Development

___ Shows hand preference (which is _____)
___ Turns with hand easily (knobs, lids, eggbeaters)
___ Pours liquid into glass without spilling
___ Unfastens and fastens zippers, buttons, Velcro tabs
___ Picks up and inserts objects with ease
___ Uses drawing/writing tools with control
___ Uses scissors with control
___ Pounds in nail with control

7. Cognitive Development: Classification and Seriation

___ Recognizes basic geometric shapes
___ Recognizes colors
___ Recognizes differences in size
___ Sorts objects by appearance
___ Discriminates things that are alike from those that are different
___ Puts parts together to make a whole
___ Arranges events in sequence from first to last
___ Arranges objects in series according to a certain rule

8. Cognitive Development: Number, Time, Space, Memory

___ Counts by rote to ten
___ Counts objects to ten
___ Knows the daily schedule in sequence
___ Knows what happened yesterday
___ Can build a block enclosure

___ Can locate an object behind or beside something
___ Recalls words to songs, chants
___ Can recollect and act on a series of directions

9. Spoken Language

___ Speaks confidently in the classroom
___ Speaks clearly enough for adults to understand
___ Speaks in expanded sentences
___ Takes part in conversations with other children
___ Asks questions with proper word order
___ Makes negative responses with proper word order
___ Uses past tense verbs correctly
___ Plays with rhyming words

10. Written Language

___ Pretends to write by making scribbling
___ Includes features of real letters in scribbling
___ Identifies own written name
___ Identifies classroom labels
___ Knows some alphabet letters
___ Makes real letters
___ Prints letters of name
___ Prints name correctly in linear manner

11. Art Skills

___ Makes random marks or covers paper with color
___ Scribbles on paper
___ Forms basic shapes
___ Makes markings
___ Makes suns

___ Draws humans as circles with arms and legs attached
___ Draws animals, trees
___ Makes pictorial drawings

12. Imagination

___ Pretends by replaying familiar routines
___ Needs particular props to do pretend play
___ Assigns roles or takes assigned roles
___ May switch roles without warning
___ Uses language for creating and sustaining plot
___ Uses exciting, danger-packed themes
___ Takes on characteristics and action related to role
___ Uses elaborate and creative themes, ideas, details

PSYCHOLOGICAL AND BEHAVIORAL DEVELOPMENT OF CHILDREN

(Reprint from Brennemann's Practice of Pediatrics, Published by Harper and Row, 1977)

Justin D. Call, MD

BIRTH TO AGE 1 MONTH

Areas for Routine Observation and Inquiry

1. Feeding, anticipatory behavior, holding position, play
2. Spontaneous visual activity
3. Reflexes: rooting, grasp, head prone, startle, suck, and hand-mouth
4. Activity level: general, hand-mouth
5. Hand use
6. Response to stimuli when alert
7. Sleep pattern

Landmarks of Normal Psychologic Development

1. Holds head up in prone position
2. Anticipatory behavior at feeding
3. Visual fixation and visual following beyond the midline
4. Stops crying with novel stimulus, holding, or rocking
5. Intact vigorous sucking activity in regular bursts
6. Alert response to light and sound
7. Begins to play after feeding
8. Holds on with his hands to whatever is available during early part of feeding

Common Parental Concerns Usually Not Problems

1. Prefers eating every two hours
2. Prickly heat rash
3. Not satisfied with feeding
4. Wants to be held "all the time"
5. Grunts with red face during BMs
6. Sucking fingers or thumb

Typical Signs of Psychologic Disturbance

1. Failure to gain weight
2. Excessive spitting up
3. No eye contact
4. Failure to hold head up
5. Failure to show anticipatory behavior at feedingtime
6. Failure to hold on with hands
7. Ticlike movements of face and head

Landmarks of Normal Psychologic Development

1. Social smile with mother
2. Many social games with mother and other family member
3. Quietness, immobile face, and subdued affectomotor responses to stranger
4. Voluntary hand use
5. Voice plus play overtures actively inviting reciprocity with mother
6. Sleeps through night
7. Patterned mealtime

Common Parental Concerns Usually Not Problems

1. Constipation
2. Demands for attention
3. Prefers to be propped up
4. Spoiled
5. Teething-biting
6. Sucking fingers or thumb

Typical Signs of Psychologic Disturbance

1. Persistent sleep problem
2. Hyperactivity and hyperresponsiveness
3. Wheezing without infection
4. Lack of interest in social stimuli
5. Does not enjoy upright position
6. Excessive rocking of self (other than or when alone)

AGE 2 TO 3 MONTHS

Areas for Routine Observation and Inquiry

1. Play with mother
2. Smiling response with mother and strangers
3. Sleep and activity patterns
4. Feeding
5. Response to stimuli
6. Hand use

Landmarks of Normal Psychologic Development

1. Social smile with mother, with strangers and with face mask
2. Social games ending with smiles
3. Oral imitation (cough game)

4. Controls breast or bottle with hands
5. Midline hand use
6. Prolonged visual tracking

Common Parental Concerns Usually Not Problems

1. Irritable crying
2. Colic
3. Constipation
4 Not sleeping through night
5. Sucking fingers or thumb

Typical Signs of Psychologic Disturbance

1. Failure to thrive
2. Indifference to social stimuli, e.g., human face, voice, and play overtures
3. Persistent hyperactivity and sleep disturbance
4. Vomiting and diarrhea with physical illness
5. Hyperresponsiveness or hyporesponsiveness to stimuli

AGE 4 TO 6 MONTHS

Areas for Routine Observation and Inquiry

1. Play with mother
2. Smiling response with mother, with strangers
3. Sleep and activity pattern
4. Feeding
5. Response to stimuli
6. Hand use

Common Parental Concerns Usually Not Problems

Common Parental Concerns Usually Not Problems

1. Dropping things
2. Messy feeding
3. Disrupted sleep associated with teething move to new home, or illness
4. "Temper"

Typical Signs of Psychologic Disturbance

1. Persistent sleep problem
2. Eating problems, e.g., refusing to use hands or hold glass, very limited diet.
3. Unpatterned sleep and eating (lack of predictability)
4. Lack of imitation of simple sounds, gestures, of facial expressions
5. Lack of affect
6. Bizarre play
7. Low socialization
8. Lack of distress with strangers
9. Excessive self-stimulation and self-destructive behavior
10. Rumination (i.e., swallowing of regurgitated food)
11. Withholding of BMs
12. Apathy
13. Anaclitic depression

AGE 7 TO 9 MONTHS

Areas for Routine Observation and Inquiry

1. Play with mother
2. Smiling response with mother, not with Strangers

3. Sleep and activity patterns
4. Feeding
5. Response to stimuli
6. Hand use
7. Response to solid food
8. Self-feeding
9. Negative affectomotor response to separation from mother
10. Response to strange places
11. Relationship with siblings

Landmarks of Normal Psychologic Development

1. Mild separation anxiety
2. Subtlety in affectomotor responses and in smile
3. "Dada" or "Mama"
4. Hand use
5. Use of "executive finger" (extended index finger in touching and exploring objects)

Landmarks of Normal Psychologic Development

1. Walks
2. Reaches out for grasps and manipulates familiar and strange objects
3. Attentive to parent
4. Stops and then goes ahead while saying "no"
5. Plays and imitations increase
6. Problem solving and investigation increase

Common Parental Concerns Usually Not Problems

1. Getting into things: climbing

2. Constipation
3. Declining appetite
4. Self-feeding and being fed
5. Screaming
6. Mild tantrums
7. Attachment to transitional object

Typical Signs of Psychologic Disturbance

1. No words
2. Sleep problems
3. Withdrawn behavior
4. Excessive rocking, posturing
5. Bizarre play
6. No separation distress
7. Night wandering
8. Excessive distractibility
9. Bowel disturbances

AGE 10 TO 15 MONTHS

Areas for Routine Observation and Inquiry

1. Play with mother
2. Smiling response with mother, not with strangers
3. Sleep and activity patterns
4. Feeding
5. Response to stimuli
6. Response to solid food
7. Self-feeding
8. Response from separation from mother and reunion

9. Response to strange places
10. Relationship with siblings
11. Interest in exploratory behavior when conditions are optimal
12. Manipulative behavior
13. Behavioral limits
14. Speech, words, sounds, and names
15. Plans for trips and separation: babysitters

Typical Signs of Psychologic Disturbance

1. No speech
2. Excessive body rocking
3. Inappropriate play
4. Withholding and other bowel problems
5. Sleep disturbance
6. Retarded development or persistent regression

AGE 16 MONTHS TO 2 YRS

Areas for Routine Observation and Inquiry

1. Speech development
2. Play
3. Eating, sleeping, and toilet training
4. Response to strangers
5. Response to separation
6. Limits for mobility and aggressive behavior

Landmarks of Normal Psychologic Development

1. Say "no" and responds with "no"

2. Use of about 20 words
3. Primary feminine identification, both girls and boys (e.g., interest in dress, shoes, baby)
4. Separates from parent and reports back
5. Microcosmic play (solitary play with small objects)
6. Imitation of vocal inflection
7. Enjoys and makes use of new experience when conditions are optimal

Common Parental Concerns Usually Not Problems

1. Getting into things: climbing
2. Stubbornness
3. Temper out bursts
4. Upset easily
5. Stuttering
6. Sibling rivalry
7. Won't try new foods
8. Regressive behavior with illness or stress
9. Wants own way and fusses
10. Temper tantrums occasionally
11. Short-lived unreasonable fears

Typical sign of Psychologic Disturbance

1. Disturbed sleep animal dreams
2. Persistent soiling or enuresis
3. Persistent eating problems
4. Non-speaking (beyond 18 months)
5. Inappropriate play
6. Fears of dark, ghosts, burglars, shyness
7. Excessively body rocking, finger sucking, and tics

AGE 25 MONTHS TO 3 YRS

Areas for Routine Observation and Inquiry

1. Sibling and peer relations
2. Speech
3. Nursery school
4. Toileting
5. Play preference
6. Limits, discipline, and daily routine
7. Dreams and night terrors, fears
8. Areas of interest and skills

Landmarks of Normal Psychologic Development

1. Parallel play (appropriate play alongside of peers) (2½ years)
2. Collateral peer play (3 years)
3. Bedtime ritual (including transitional object)
4. Cooperative play (4 years)
5. Two- and three-word speech (use of speech as a tool to make things happen) (2 years)
6. Creative use of speech (for reflection organization) (3 to 4 years)
7. Successful toilet training (2 to 2½ years)
8. Accepts reasonable limits (2 to 2½ years)
9. Special skills and talent (3 to 4 years
10. Talks to self (2½ years)
11. " What's this?" (in reference to new objects)

Common Parental Concerns Usually Not Problems

1. Messy play
2. Stuttering

3. Won't put things away
4. Aggressive and possessive play
5. Occasional soiling or wetting
6. Stubbornness
7. Won't try new foods

Typical sign of Psychologic Disturbance

1. Disturbed sleep animal dreams
2. Persistent soiling or enuresis
3. Persistent eating problems
4. Non-speaking (beyond 18 months)
5. Inappropriate play
6. Fears of dark, ghosts, burglars, shyness
7. Excessive body rocking, finger sucking, and tics

AGE 37 MONTHS TO 4 YRS

Areas for Routine Observation and Inquiry

1. Sibling and peer relations
2. Speech
3. Nursery school
4. Toilet
5. Play preferences
6. Limits disciplines and daily routine
7. Dreams and night terrors, fears
8. Areas of interest and skills

Landmarks of Normal Psychologic Development

1. Cooperative play with peers
2. Sibling truce

3. Creative use of speech: "3-year prose"
4. Special skills and talents, e.g., painting manipulation skills, dance, music
5. Some leadership capacity in group

Common Parental Concerns Usually Not Problems

1. Messy play
2. Stuttering
3. Won't put things away
4. Aggressive and possessive play
5. Occasional soiling or wetting
6. Stubbornness
7. Won't try new foods
8. Regressive behavior with illness or stress
9. Wants own way and fusses
10. Temper tantrums occasionally
11. Short-lived unreasonable fears
12. Jealousy
13. Excessive reveries

Typical Signs of Psychologic Disturbance

1. Bowel and urinary problems
2. Lying
3. Persistent fearfulness regarding school, other children, and new situations
4. Finickiness with food
5. Persistent phobias
6. Overdependence
7. Fire setting
8. Pseudomaturity
9. Running away

10. Nonadaptive neatness
11. Persistent thumb sucking
12. Strange, bizarre, or withdrawn behavior
13. Uncommunicativeness
14. Cruelty to animals
15. No friends
16. Lack of interest in appearance or developing skills
17. Disturbed sleep and frightening dreams
18. Persistently upset by changes
19. Excessive clinging to transitional objects

AGE 5 TO 7 YEARS

Areas for Routine Observation and Inquiry

1. Entrance into school
2. Peer relations
3. Family relationships, particularly with father
4. Academic performance
5. Class behavior
6. Interests and skills, likes and dislikes
7. Physical abilities
8. TV viewing habits
9. Sleep and dreams
10. Sexual interests
11. Play
12. Life space
13. Daily routine
14. Self-care
15. Care of belongings

Landmarks of Normal Psychologic Developing

1. Capacity for group orientation and membership
2. At ease away from home for part of the day (some concerns at night)
3. Interest in father's work
4. Early learning skills; knows right from wrong in categorical terms
5. Can play catch well and solve simple puzzles
6. More detailed dreams (silly and complicated)
7. Interest in procreation
8. On the make
9. Has clear preferences for friends, TV, clothes activities, and use of free time
10. Appropriate sex identity is clear

Common Parental Concerns Usually Not Problems

1. Takes things and doesn't always share
2. Doesn't always mind
3. Poor tables manners
4. Prefers play to school and work
5. Very active
6. Oversensitive to criticism
7. Timid with unfamiliar people
8. Short-lived (2 week)
9. Occasionally somber
10. Occasionally negative
11. Temper outbursts

AGE 8 TO 10 YEARS

Areas For Routine Observation and Inquiry

1. Peer relations
2. Family relationships, particularly with father
3. Academic performance
4. Class behavior
5. Interests and skills, likes and dislikes
6. Physical abilities
7. TV viewing habits
8. Sleep and dreams
9. Sexual interests
10. Play
11. Life space
12. Daily routine
13. Self-care
14. Care of belongings
15. Reading skills
16. Reasoning ability
17. Ability to tell jokes
18. Play with words

Landmarks of Normal Psychologic Development

1. Learns to read and enjoys reading (by third grade)
2. Has special friends of same sex
3. Belongs to groups of friends
4. Knows rules of games and enforces them
5. Uses "scientific" observation approach to new situations
6. Enjoys travel

7. Knows right from wrong, with some contingencies and conditions
8. Shuns identification with opposite sex
9. Tells truth or avoids speaking rather than tell a lie

Common Parental Concerns Usually Not Problems

1. Aggressive self-assertive behavior
2. Talking back
3. Moodiness
4. Temper
5. Secretiveness

Typical Signs of Psychologic Disturbance

1. Running away
2. School failure
3. No friends
4. Persistent fears
5. Withdrawal
6. Persistent fickiness with food
7. Immaturity
8. Pseudomaturity
9. Nonadaptive obsessional behavior
10. Recurrent nightmares
11. Language and speech problems
12 Toileting and bowel problems
13. Hallucinations
14. Tics

www.ingramcontent.com/pod-product-compliance
Lightning Source LLC
Chambersburg PA
CBHW020945230426
43666CB00005B/183